Asperger Syndrome and Psychotherapy

of related interest

Asperger's Syndrome
A Guide for Parents and Professionals
Tony Attwood
ISBN 1 85302 577 1

Freaks, Geeks and Asperger Syndrome
A User Guide to Adolescence
Luke Jackson
ISBN 1 84310 098 3

Relationship Development Intervention with Children,
Adolescents and Adults
Social and Emotional Development Activities
for Asperger Syndrome, Autism, PDD and NLD
Steven E. Gutstein and Rachelle K. Sheely
ISBN 1 84310 717 1

Playing, Laughing and Learning with Children
on the Autism Spectrum
A Practical Resource of Play Ideas for Parents and Carers
Julia Moor
ISBN 1 84310 060 6

Addressing the Challenging Behavior
of Children with High-Functioning Autism / Asperger
Syndrome in the Classroom
A Guide for Teachers and Parents
Rebecca A. Moyes
ISBN 1 84310 719 8

Pretending to be Normal
Living with Asperger's Syndrome
Liane Holliday Willey
ISBN 1 85302 749 9

Asperger Syndrome and Psychotherapy
Understanding Asperger Perspectives

Paula Jacobsen

Jessica Kingsley Publishers
London and New York

First published in the United Kingdom in 2003
by Jessica Kingsley Publishers Ltd
116 Pentonville Road
London N1 9JB, England
and
29 West 35th Street, 10th fl.
New York, NY 10001-2299

www.jkp.com

Copyright © Paula Jacobsen 2003

Library of Congress Cataloging in Publication Data
A CIP catalog record for this book is available from the Library of Congress

British Library Cataloguing in Publication Data
A CIP catalogue record for this book is available from the British Library

ISBN 1 84310 743 0

Printed and Bound in Great Britain by
Athenaeum Press, Gateshead, Tyne and Wear

Contents

Acknowledgments

The knowledge I have about Asperger Syndrome comes from the children and parents in my clinical practice. I am very thankful and appreciative for all that we have learned together.

I first heard about theory of mind and central coherence from Linda Lotspeich. These are the concepts that seemed to make sense of many aspects of the thinking and behavior of those with Asperger's. In my clinical work, I used these concepts with children and adults as we worked together to understand the Asperger mind.

Parents in my practice and I have developed intervention plans that have evolved, as we use them. Pam Ehrlich prepared a working model of the Reference Binder. I appreciate these contributions and have included some samples in the Appendices.

This book was written because of my participation in something that was initially quite unrelated to my work with Asperger Syndrome. Cleo Eulau is a distinguished clinical social worker. She has served as a teacher, supervisor, mentor and role model to countless mental health professionals. Cleo was the head of social work in the Child Psychiatry Department at Stanford for many years, has taught at Smith College, has been in private practice for many years, and serves on the Voluntary Clinical Faculty of the Stanford University School of Medicine as a Clinical Professor. In 1994, the Cleo Eulau Center (CEC) was founded and named for Cleo, who has been a participant in, and advisor to, the agency. The mission of the CEC is to help children and adolescents who have experienced adversity to grow to become competent adults. I have been an advisor to the agency since its inception. This was an opportunity for me to participate as a volunteer to an agency that served children who were unlikely to be seen by therapists in private practice.

In 1996, Candace Pierce became director of the agency, and I participated in discussions and later in a study group that developed a school consultation intervention to address the agency's goals. Research about resiliency speaks powerfully to a strengths perspective and the impact of relationships on positive psychological development. We developed a school Resiliency Consultant role, based on recognition of the importance of a child's relationship with a teacher, and the ability to impact many children through teachers and schools.

Cleo has always been dedicated to the continuing education of professionals working with children, and she wanted the agency to provide continuing education. Cleo knew that I had a strengths-based approach in my work with Asperger's. She encouraged my developing continuing education programs focused on clinical practice with Asperger Syndrome. One was a twelve-hour symposium for experienced child psychotherapists. In preparing, I developed my notes and outlines more completely. A good part of this book was written for my Cleo Eulau Center presentations. In other words, much of it was written before I knew that I was writing a book. I am very sure that I would never have written a book, otherwise.

Susan Greenberg-Englander and Bob Levit are my colleagues of many years who have consistently supported me. They read my manuscript, as did Julie Lee-Ancajas. Susan brought the perspective of a psycho-dynamically trained adult psychiatrist. Bob brought the perspective of a psychodynamically trained child psychologist. They raised questions and made comments that helped me to say what I was trying to say, more clearly. Julie brought the perspective of someone who was very familiar with Asperger Syndrome and Nonverbal Learning Disorders. She helped me to address the difficulty that therapists trained in a deficit model will face in focusing on "who the person is," rather than focusing on the deficits. Linda Lotspeich also read my manuscript and made general comments. I am appreciative of the time and energy they all gave to this, and for their thoughtful and helpful comments. My publisher, Jessica Kingsley, was enthusiastic about this book from the beginning. Her observations, from the perspective of the potential reader, enabled me to easily re-write several chapters, to present more clearly what I wanted to communicate. I also want to thank my husband, Warren, for his consistent support and his patience through this project.

Preface

A person's perspective is the way in which that individual interprets the meaning of his or her experiences. From my clinical work, I know that learning the perspective of my patients is the foundation of a strengths-based approach to understanding and mastery. This is true of those with Asperger Syndrome, and it is basic to my understanding of them and my work with them. Those with Asperger Syndrome are often described as having difficulty understanding the perspective of others. Yet I have found that the challenge for us, and the key to this work, is our understanding of their perspective. It is not easy to set aside our meanings and hear what something means to someone whose thought processes and references are very different from our own.

Some readers may be very familiar with the Autism – Pervasive Development Disorders (PDD) – Asperger spectrum. They may easily see cognitive and social deficits in the people I describe. Clearly, those are present. For those readers, it may not be easy to attend to seeing who these people *are*, rather than who they are not.

I find that I can best explain and illustrate what I have learned by using many case examples. It is my hope that these examples will allow the reader to recognize familiar people and situations, and to understand them from the perspective of the person with Asperger's. The case material has been disguised. Some vignettes are from my work with a specific child or other family member. In those cases, I have permission to use the material. Some behaviors and interactions that I describe have occurred in similar ways with several children. Some vignettes and case descriptions are a compilation of several people with whom I have worked.

Part One

Clinical Work with Asperger Syndrome

1

Learning from Those
who Have Asperger Syndrome

Diagnosis is not Enough

The treatment of children and adults with Asperger Syndrome is not traditional psychotherapy. There are differences in the direct work as well as in the collateral work with family members. For children and adolescents, there is often a greater need for collaborative contacts with schools and with other professionals. The therapy and the collaboration are very specific to the difficulties and abilities that their strengths and their challenges present.

Formal diagnosis of any mental disorder relies on a description of what is observable, of how the person presents as we look from the outside. Asperger Syndrome is included in the American Psychiatric Association *Diagnostic and Statistical Manual of Mental Disorders* (DSM-IV). This manual provides a description of observable behavior and symptoms, the purpose of which is to enable clinicians and others to refer to agreed upon criteria. Understanding deficits tells us more about who someone is not, rather than who someone is.

Nonverbal Learning Disorder is not included in the Diagnostic Manual at this time. However, it is a diagnosis that is used by child therapists and educators. Some of the features of Nonverbal Learning Disorder are very similar to those of Asperger Syndrome. Many children who are diagnosed with Asperger Syndrome have a Nonverbal Learning Disorder. These children often have similar or overlapping issues, dynamics, and needs. For purpose of their clinical presentation, I have included some examples of children diagnosed with Nonverbal Learning Disorder when their issues and abilities are similar to those of children with an Asperger Syndrome diagnosis. Some clinicians and researchers consider Asperger Syndrome and Nonverbal

Learning diagnoses to be a level of autism. Dr Linda Lotspeich of the Neuropsychiatry PDD Clinic at the Stanford University Department of Psychiatry and Behavioral Sciences has suggested that it is possible that someday we may just address the question of how much autism is present. This would require general knowledge and acceptance that autism is a spectrum, and not always a very debilitating disorder (Lotspeich 2001).

Many clinicians want to understand the psychodynamics of a patient, a look at the inside that gives meaning to the observable behavior. While traditional psychodynamic theory does not help us understand much of what we see in Asperger Syndrome, it may help us to understand some of our responses to these people. The dynamics of a person with Asperger Syndrome can be best understood by addressing cognitive issues such as theory of mind, executive functioning, and central coherence. I will explore these.

The description in the current Diagnostic Manual and diagnostic formulations generally are based on a deficit model. Speaking diagnostically can mean emphasizing deficits and describing observable behaviors as symptoms from a deficit perspective. In a therapeutic relationship, the work is often based on understanding what we would call symptoms and deficits from the perspective of their meaning to the person we are seeing. From this perspective the symptoms can be seen as an attempt at mastery of something difficult. This enables us to be more conscious of, and to articulate, that part of our work that recognizes and enhances growth. In individual psychotherapy, knowing the patient is much more than determining a diagnostic label or psychodynamic formulation. It includes understanding, as best we can, that person's subjective experience.

Let's Start Where I Started

I want to begin by sharing with you how I came to know children and adults with Asperger Syndrome and Nonverbal Learning Disorders. Perhaps, if you are a psychotherapist, a language therapist, an occupational therapist, a teacher, a parent or other family member, or even an adult with Asperger Syndrome (or many aspects of Asperger Syndrome), you may recognize some of the situations and experiences that I describe.

Whenever I address how I came to know these people, I find myself thinking about what is always important if we are to understand another person. We have to be open to knowing that person's experience from his or her perspective. We cannot only know someone from the perspective of our training, our theoretical orientation, or from the perspective of our own thinking and our own lives. This is especially true, and much more important, when we do not share many of the same references and thought processes. It can be very tempting, but is not necessarily accurate or useful, to attribute what would be our own meanings and intentions to the behavior of others.

Learning from the Children

Long before Asperger's and Nonverbal Learning Disorder diagnoses were used by child psychotherapists, I saw these children in my practice. They, along with their parents, became my teachers. I knew about psychodynamics, about unconscious motivation, about the subtle or "understood" meanings of verbal and nonverbal language. What I knew about these things was not helping me to know these people's minds and experiences. Their behavior or comments sometimes seemed self-centered or detached, uncaring or even hurtful. Yet I could see that they were often very attached to important people in their lives. In addition, they could be very happy when they pleased others, and unhappy when they disappointed others. However, why another person was pleased or disappointed was often a mystery to them. They were sometimes aware that they seemed odd to others, and others often seemed odd to them. It's my job, I may tell a child, to understand him, and I need the child's help to do this. I know that I cannot expect children to understand my mind and my references so that we can communicate. I must understand them first. With these particular children that was a formidable task. Yet recognizing it, recognizing that understanding those children's minds was *my* task, freed me to do just that. I did not need to help them change, to help them become more acceptable. First, I needed to learn who they were. The process of doing that often became central to the treatment. As we understood their meanings, their experiences, and their thoughts, changes in understanding and increased mastery often occurred, as also often happens in more traditional psychotherapy.

These children had strengths, intense interests, and an amazing memory for a great deal of information. Often they were very good at logic, at linear reasoning. They seemed to have a different kind of brain. Rather than having conscious or unconscious motivation, they were often oblivious to their own actions and the effect of their actions or statements on others. When their play was "pretend" play, it was not projective, not symbolic of their internal processes, feelings, or conflicts. The mind of the other was an enigma to them. When we spoke, I found that we were not necessarily in the same conversation. Their play, if they did play, did not tell me about them in the way that the neurotypical child's play does. In our work, I had to engage in a conscious process of understanding and articulating the child's perspective. This very process, I realized much later, brought conscious awareness to them of their own mind and another mind. The "aha" of understanding was not an emotional experience for them, although it might reduce their anxiety; it was an "aha" of intellectual understanding. For them, intellectual knowledge formed the basis for understanding how to deal with the world around them.

I looked for a frame of reference to help me understand my role with these children, a way to understand our relationship that would have meaning to me. Although I recognize that this is not a true analogy to the Asperger experience with neurotypicals, the analogy that seemed to work was one in which I might find myself in the "alien" role. If I were to try to live in a very different culture, as I tried to learn what is appropriate, I might constantly commit faux pas. I would undoubtedly be misunderstood, behave in ways that seemed inappropriate or offensive, and I would misunderstand others. I would need to learn new skills, rules, and the meaning of my behavior to others.

Whom would I want to have help me, as I struggled to do this? If my guide were someone from that culture, I would need to have that person know and be able to describe that culture in a way that I could understand. It would be more supportive, and less lonely, if that person were also understanding of me and of my experiences and frustrations. It would help if that guide were interested in me and my perspective, and respected it as a valid experience. I would want to find a way to be with others that worked, without trying to become one of them, which I could not do. That is the kind of person I need to be in my relationship with those with Asperger's. From that perspective, I can work to understand the valid experience of those with Asperger's, as well as the need for them to develop awareness of the perspective of others.

David

Many years ago, I saw a boy who today would be diagnosed with Asperger Syndrome. David was a very bright seven-year-old, but had no friends or close relationships outside the family. His parents referred him because he was anxious, isolated, and very unhappy at school. In addition, he sometimes got extremely angry when frustrated, confused, or overwhelmed. Recess, in particular, was difficult for him, and he dreaded it. During recess the children, most of whom had known each other for years, socialized or played sports activities. He was not interested in sports and often was confused during group activities.

David had specific interests and learned everything he could about these subjects. He had difficulty with sustained eye contact, and some awkward motor movements and habits, such as those that some autistic children exhibit. Yet he was not autistic, as I understood autism then. He loved to talk in detail about his experiences, but responded with anger or withdrew when others were uninterested, became bored, or otherwise reacted negatively.

David attended an alternative school with a nurturing atmosphere and a developmental approach. It was not structured enough for him. His parents had always been committed to providing a child-centered, developmental, school experience for their children. Yet this school did not feel safe to him. It was with difficulty, but with understanding of his enormous need for concrete, predictable structure, that they placed him in another school. The new school was agreed to select teachers with structured classrooms and clear expectations, yet a willingness to be accepting of this bright but unusual child. Both the school and David's family worked to accept some of his odd interests and behavior.

David liked to share information and experiences. He was only able to do that by including every detail. Once, after a long family vacation, David drew a map of the countries they had visited. In each town there was a church, and he climbed to the top of the tower whenever that was possible. Although they were away for many weeks, when he returned he knew the name of every town and every church tower. It might be tempting to attribute symbolic meaning to David's "tower collection." For him, however, this interest organized his trip around something identifiable and nameable that occurs predictably, in even the smallest of towns. He also knew the location of the train stations they used and the names or numbers of the trains they took between the cities and towns they visited.

David loved my listening to his very detailed information, clearly unable to summarize in any way that felt satisfactory to him. He did know that my willingness to hear every detail was based on its importance to him and his wish to share, and he tolerated that. I answered him honestly about my interest. He knew that some of the information was interesting to me. He also knew that I was happy to hear the details, but only because he wanted to share them with me. I noted and wanted to understand his ability to remember. I wanted to know what was in his mind. Did he see the map in his mind with all the locations? It became clear to both of us that my mind was different from his. Yet we accepted each other.

Although I saw him for several years in play therapy, David did not ever engage in meaningful projective play. Sometimes we played skill board games that he mastered. Logic and understanding strategy were strengths. At one point he became interested in a board game called The Ungame (Ungame Company 1975). This is a game in which there is no winner or loser and no particular goal or end. The game is played by rolling a die and landing on one of three types of squares: "Tell it like it is," "Do your own thing," and "Hang Up!" For "Tell it like it is" we had to take a card and answer the question on it. The questions were often about feelings, people, preferences, or wishes, such as: "WHEN DO YOU FEEL SAD?" "DESCRIBE A GOOD NEIGHBOR," "WHAT IS YOUR FAVORITE FOOD?" and "WHAT WOULD YOU DO IF YOU HAD A 'MAGIC WAND'?" For "Do your own thing" we could tell something or ask each other a question.

Initially, David looked for "right answers." He tried to answer factually and often answered as concretely as possible. Rather than providing a way to explore his own feelings or worries, as it might have for a more typical child, this game provided a way to recognize and explore more than one possible meaning of a question, and more than one possible answer. I found myself articulating my observations of each of our thoughts in a way that I never would have with most of the children I saw.

"Hang Up!" squares included directions such as: "If you felt lonely this week, take a vacation at CHEERFUL CHALET," "If you worried this week, relax on WORRY WHARF," and "If you feel happy now, go to HAPPY HOUSE." David learned the psychological meaning of the expression "hang up" in this game. He had not heard the expression used this way before. He took a toy telephone, put the receiver to his ear, and then slammed it down. "This is 'Hang Up!'," he said. "That is another kind of 'hang up'," I responded, and we both laughed. This was funny the first time he did it, but David continued to do this every time he landed on a "Hang Up!" square, every time we played this game. He seemed to enjoy doing it. He also seemed to continue to find it funny every time, and laughed after he did it.

While David could continue to do this with me, it would have been seen as very inappropriate in any other setting. It also seemed inappropriate for me to go along with it, as though it was an expected kind of behavior, without some comment. It took time and thought for me to feel I could comfortably make him aware, without sounding as if I were saying his behavior was wrong and I was correcting him. Finally, I commented that doing this seemed funny to him and fun to do. He really seemed to want to do it every time. For me, it was funny the first time, and it might be funny to remember a time or two, but after that it did not seem funny any more. That is why I did not laugh. We agreed that he could continue to do this when we played, just because we both understood that it was important to him. This was his therapy. It should be fine for him to play the way he likes here.

David liked riddles and knock-knock jokes. These often were based on the understanding of a concrete play on words. He could get "stuck" on a particular riddle or joke that he liked, and he would want to tell it over and over. He liked me to find new jokes for him, and then would respond by sharing one he had previously told me. Of course, I knew the answer or punch line already. One favorite was:

David: Knock-knock.

Paula: Who's there?

David: Boo.

Paula: Boo who?

David: You don't have to cry about it!

David had told me this joke a couple of times. When he told it once again, at the end of a session, I said, "You know, David, I do know 'who's there'. Would you like me to pretend I don't know, so you can tell me again?" He said he did, but was clearly thinking about it. We went through it again, but this time with both of us consciously aware that this was different from telling a new joke. He was repeating something because he liked to, and I was participating because it was important to him. Verbalizing this process allowed him to continue, but made the experience that each of us had more conscious and overt.

David was learning about his own behavior and preferences, and that they could be recognized and accepted. He already knew that what he said and did was often seen as inappropriate and not acceptable in many situations. In part, this was because what was comfortable for him might not be comfortable for others. We could talk about that, too. We did not examine what he did from a perspective of right or wrong. It was about the differences in what people preferred, differences in what made them comfortable or uncomfortable.

As I worked with David, I realized that he was recognizing and thinking about his own and others' thoughts and experiences. He was studying them, much as he would study any other subject. This was the hardest "subject" he was studying. He could not master it in his preferred way, by memorizing all there was to know about the facts or by straightforward logic.

John

Another child whom I saw years ago was referred by his parents and his pediatrician for depression and difficulty dealing with frustration. He was intelligent and had learned all the basic factual knowledge in the early grades without any problem. As a fourth grader, he was resisting or refusing to do his homework. He said it was "stupid" and he became very frustrated as his parents sat with him or urged him to do his assignments. He did not want to pay attention to his work. His parents and his pediatrician wondered if he had an Attention Deficit Disorder. They gave him a trial of a stimulant medication. At first they thought it was helping, but it soon became obvious that it was not. An increase in dosage made things worse, not better, so they discontinued it.

One day John became even more upset than usual at homework time. He started sobbing. Then he said he was going to kill himself and ran out of the house. His parents were very concerned and scoured the neighborhood for quite a while before they finally found him. That is when their pediatrician referred him for a clinical assessment.

When I first met John, he told me something several other children have told me. He informed me that he was from another planet. He did not seem particularly distressed or sad as he told me this. He did not present it with affect. He knew it was my job to get to know him – his parents and I had told him that. He told me in the same manner and tone as he told me his age, his grade in school, his interests, and the names of his siblings and friends. It was information.

As John saw that I was listening and wanted to understand him and his experience of his world, he became less depressed. However, I began to realize that when I thought I knew what he was talking about, I often made incorrect assumptions. We were not really in the same conversation. Our references were not the same. If we figured this out, it was not funny, the way it usually is when two people realize they are not talking about the same thing. We have all had the experience of participating in a conversation that seemed to hang together for a while and then became confusing. At some point we clarify that one of us was still referring to one thing while the other thought we were referring to something else. When we figure that out, it seems funny and we both laugh. I understood much later that we only find these misunderstandings funny when we recognize our own and the other person's thoughts. We understand both references at the same time. This did not happen with John. When a misunderstanding occurred, we might clear it up, but he had little or no understanding of how the misunderstanding occurred, and it did not seem very funny to him.

John was very bright, yet unless expectations were explained specifically and in detail, he felt overwhelmed. When he said that he did not understand what his teacher wanted in many assignments, it was true. Even if he could do the work, he did not understand what was important to his teacher. Literature was especially difficult for him. He needed information to be factual or logical, and explained clearly and concretely.

Once, John became very angry about a literature book he was supposed to read. He had to read it, because it was a required, assigned reading for his entire class. John tried to start reading the first page a couple of times. He threw the book down, and he told his mother the book did not make any sense. His mother wanted to understand what did not make sense. "It's the most stupid book written. None of it makes sense," he told her. When she asked him to help her understand or show her the problem, he angrily took the book and read the first page out loud. There were references to several people and events that were not explained. He asked, in a furious and sarcastic tone, who this or that person was and what this or that referenced event was. "Do you think that those might be the very questions the author wants you to have?" his mother asked. "Then you can find the answers as you keep reading." His mother's guidance helped John go on with his reading, but he still thought that was a very bad way to write. He likes books that give answers and information, not books that hint at things to come.

John had difficulty in communication, because he often did not notice or understand pragmatic language, the nonverbal and the implied verbal references in communication. He began language therapy with a therapist who understood that his exceptional expressive and receptive language abilities were not adequate for the pragmatic aspects of communication as they applied to reading and written work at school as well as interpersonal communication.

Trying to figure out what he and I meant was often a part of our work. Together we would try to figure out what others may have meant, too. Although he was not eligible for special services from the school district, I collaborated with the teacher and other school personnel to "translate" the meaning of some of his statements and reactions.

Once, John's teacher was absent for more than a week. When she came back, she told the class she was very sad. Her child had had a serious infection. It resulted in neurological damage that permanently impaired her vision.

Someone asked how that could happen, and she shared the medical explanation. My patient listened attentively, visualizing and comprehending the explanation, and then said, "Wow, cool!" Other children and the teacher were shocked and upset, and the teacher called his parents and me.

John did not think it was "cool" that the child lost vision. He thought the explanation of how the body works was "cool." He needed me to know this – to know what was in his mind. We had to figure out what went wrong – what was in the mind of his teacher and some of the children. They thought he meant that her loss of vision was cool. He accepted that explanation of their misunderstanding. The teacher and children were wrong about what he meant, but he did understand what they thought and why. We figured out together, and he accepted that when someone is telling about sad feelings it is probably not a good time to focus on the facts. That person could then think (wrongly, perhaps) that you just do not care about his or her feelings.

However, John needed something more. He wanted me to see, to understand, what he thought was cool. I could understand his perspective: knowing how the body works is "cool" (in a medical school or biology class, perhaps). I also understand that when people tell you their feelings along with information, they generally want you to focus on their feelings at that time.

Comprehending and accepting his perspective was affectively difficult for me, because it was difficult for me to relate separately to the information and the sad situation. At the same time, I could see how much he needed me to understand that he did not mean anything hurtful *and* to understand his interest in the information. It is easy to see how this issue could cause misunderstandings in social and interpersonal communication.

Academically, John found that he understood best what he figured out himself. He could not rely on help, because the explanations others gave him (based, perhaps, on their assumptions about what he already understood or could easily understand) often did not help. He did not know how to ask for the help he needed, and he did not expect the help he got to be useful. Encouragement to "just try," or repeating an explanation, made him more frustrated. Two important things happened in his therapy that helped us understand this and what to do about it.

The first time we addressed this, it involved my learning something from him. John was very good at understanding spatial relations without words. He could make very complicated origami constructions that required many folds. Once he made them a few times, he remembered how and could make them again. He demonstrated and wanted me to make them, too. We each had our paper. He wanted me to watch him and do what he did. I could do that, following him one step at a time, but it was strange to him that practicing with him was not sufficient for me to be able to produce the object later.

I had difficulty remembering how to make even simple objects that did not require very many folds. I needed the directions or a demonstration over and over. I explained this to John, and he dictated and demonstrated as I wrote down instructions and diagrams for myself. I needed to do that, if he wanted me to be able to make the same construction later. I described my process, and asked about his. I could not see the folds sequentially in my mind as he could. I needed him to be patient as I struggled to translate his demonstration into words and pictures that I would understand and be able to use later. He was able to see that my way of thinking and learning was very different from his. I needed to use his teaching in a way that I could understand at the moment and utilize later.

The second important thing that happened involved John learning something from me. John wanted to play the game Connect Four (Milton Bradley 1979) with me. Connect Four is a game that uses checkers and a vertical two-dimensional frame into which the checkers are dropped by each player in turn. The object is to connect four red or black checkers in a horizontal, vertical, or diagonal line (much like Tic Tac Toe requires connecting three Xs or Os, but with many more squares in which to place the checkers).

While I do not try very hard to win, I do not purposely lose at games, except by overt agreement with a child. The strategy in Connect Four is particularly easy for me. I try to set up my pieces in such a way that I will have two possible spaces in which to place my fourth checker in a row. If one is blocked, I can then use the other space. With minimal attention to this strategy, I almost always won. Although he accepted losing, John wanted to win. He insisted, at first, that I was probably lucky. I asked if he thought that I might have a strategy. He responded that, if I did, he did not want to hear about it. "Never mind about that," he said. He would do this himself. He tried going first. Then he tried going second. He tried using the red checkers. Then he tried using the black checkers. He tried figuring out a strategy himself and attempted several he thought might work. This went on for many weeks.

One day John came in, set up the game, and said, "Teach me your strategy." I told him it was my job to explain this so he could understand. If he did not understand, I was not explaining it well enough, and I had to find another way. I thought that I might need him to be patient with me as I tried to explain. I hoped to make it clear that I could fail the explaining; he was not failing the understanding, if my explanation was not helpful enough.

I told John that I try to have two places to win and that, for demonstration purposes, I wanted him to let me help him win so he could see what he was doing that enabled him to win. Then I essentially played both sides by talking him through his moves and having him see how this worked. We tried several ways of accomplishing the strategy. John was very excited to understand. He wanted to try it himself, and asked me to try to win. After that, he won as often as I did. John had a need to figure out the strategy by himself, because he did not expect an explanation to help. He just wanted to understand it and thought an explanation would confuse and frustrate him. It was likely to make him feel worse, more frustrated. He was not upset that he did not figure this out himself. He was happy to utilize help that he could understand.

In working with children like John, it becomes apparent how much we generally rely on shared understanding and shared ways of thinking and learning to communicate. When these fail, it is easy to see the failure as resistance or lack of desire. John knew he did not think like many other people. He often did not understand what they meant, but he also understood and could do many things that they could not easily understand or do. Perhaps that is why he thought he might be from another planet. He now had a sense of hope and a desire to understand and communicate with the earthlings around him.

While John wanted to win, he could handle losing. His resistance to learning my strategy for this game came from his expectation that my kind of explanation would not help. Sometimes children with Asperger Syndrome cannot tolerate losing a game. This can appear to be narcissistic. These children are often described as narcissistic. For practical purposes in play situations with friends, perhaps this might as well be true. Yet I found the meaning of this for the child and for planning interventions, as well as my own responses, to be quite different from the meaning with a child whose primary diagnosis was a narcissistic disorder. Let us first look at a neurotypical child with a narcissistic personality.

Eric

Eric was a five-and-a-half-year-old only child who was referred for clinical assessment and treatment. His parents described him as intelligent and capable, but noncompliant and easily angered. He had temper tantrums when life was not consistent with his expectations. He was demanding of his parents, but not emotionally close. He did not seem aware of, or concerned about, others' feelings. Eric's mother had had an extended postpartum depression. She had cared for him physically, but was not emotionally available or responsive for his first two years.

Eric's early developmental milestones were normal except language development, which was precocious, and social development, which was described as delayed. He had one neighborhood friend, but generally did not play well with other children. In preschool, he was interested in structured learning, which was easy for him, but he did not develop friendships.

During the assessment and part of the first year of treatment Eric seemed to enjoy the playroom and my attention to him. Initially he played primarily with building blocks, something he did at home. He wanted me to watch. He understood that he was coming for therapy because of his angry outbursts, and sometimes described incidents that made him angry. Eric's relationship with me was not personal. When I told him that I would be away on a vacation, after seeing him twice a week for many months, he asked if he could see someone else while I was away.

After almost a year, Eric began to play board games with me. Once he understood the concept of luck, he could play luck games expecting that each player would win some of the time. He then lost interest in these games, and only wanted to play Chinese checkers. Eric knew that Chinese checkers was a skill game, and was convinced that he could win. When he lost, he became furious with what he called his "stupid mistake." He often turned the board over, in frustration, sending marbles rolling around the room. He would not consider that an adult who has been playing all her life might be able to win this game when playing with a six-year-old, even a very smart and capable six-year-old. I invited him to think about how he might play when he is an adult who has played this game his whole life. Even the most capable six-year-old could not be expected to win against him. He disagreed. He assured me that if the six-year-old were very smart, the six-year-old would win. He would not accept any help or advantage, which I would gladly have given him. He would not allow me to agree to help him win. That would mean he was not a better player.

Eric had a greatly exaggerated sense of his superior abilities. He was enraged by a perceived failure in his own performance, because he experienced this as a narcissistic injury and could not tolerate it. He did not feel known, nor did he expect or want me to know him. No amount of understanding of the situation was useful. Eric wanted to demonstrate his superiority, and he wanted admiration. He was very aware of his anger and his tantrums at the time and afterwards. He could easily describe what he had felt and done, and he saw his behavior as a reasonable response to his situation, to the mistake he made that did not reflect his superior ability.

I finally had to stop playing Chinese checkers with Eric, because I could not figure out a way to help him that way. He informed me that it was his right to tell me what we would do, and I acknowledged that it was true that he should be able to decide what we do. However, I had failed to figure out how to help him when we played this game. Unfortunately, because of my failure to figure this out, we were going to have to find another way to work together. Eric was furious. He informed me that he was going to report me. He was not coming back unless I did what he wanted, and he planned to have me fired by the receptionist. His anger was in our relationship now. It was clearly directed towards me. His parents continued his therapy against his objections, and we began the difficult work of Eric and me both knowing and valuing him as a little boy without superior powers.

Understanding narcissism from a psychodynamic perspective was very useful to me in understanding Eric and his issues. Relying on this perspective did not help me understand the difficulty that some Asperger children have in similar situations. While many Asperger children are able to play games, even if they lose, some do have difficulty with this issue. They may become very angry, and even have tantrums, when they or their teams lose. Matt is a child who had this difficulty.

Matt

Matt was a bright, verbal seven-year-old who had long temper tantrums. He was overwhelmed by sensory stimuli, such as sounds, lights, odors, and textures. Matt was unable to control his behavior when he felt overwhelmed. He was unable to examine what had happened afterwards. He was attached to and dependent on his parents, but they could not help him at these times.

Matt learned easily by observation and reading. If he did not understand something easily, he resisted learning from or being corrected by someone else. He enjoyed mastering new skills that he figured out his own way, and did like the skills involved in playing games. However, he generally became very upset if he did not win, and could have tantrums that included turning the board over, throwing the pieces around, and raging for a half hour. He understood the concepts of luck and skill, but had almost as much trouble losing either kind of game.

At first Matt did not want me to make adjustments in the rules that would help him. However, I learned that his reason for this was that he understood changes like that to be wrong or cheating. I explained that children often allowed these changes, and it was not cheating if we both agreed to it. It was difficult for him to see that making the game easier for him than for me was not cheating. However, after a while he accepted that it was a reasonable thing for someone more experienced to do for someone less experienced, especially when the more experienced player was an adult playing with a child. I could also let him win chance games, because it seemed important to him at this time in his life, and it was not important to me. This was more difficult, but information that he could consider.

When Matt did have a tantrum, talking about it was impossible. At the time, I could see that he was so upset that language was useless. When he used language, he perseverated, and was unable to hear even the most supportive responses. When he felt better, other than our both acknowledging that he had been upset, we still could not use language to review what had happened. The reason behind this became apparent in my collaboration with the therapist of a social skills group he attended.

There were three children in Matt's social skills group. This, of course, was not a situation in which adjustments would be made to let Matt win. He was playing with peers who also wanted a chance to win. When Matt lost, he also often lost his temper. Since these tantrums could go on for a long time, his mother had to wait outside in case he had to be removed. Again, processing what happened at a later time was useless. Matt could easily say what should happen, he just could not do it in the moment. Although generally very verbal, he was unable to use language to explain or even describe what had happened.

The therapist began audiotaping Matt's social skills group. The week after he had had a long, out of control, raging tantrum, she had Matt's mother bring him in early for the next group meeting.

> "We haven't been able to figure out how to help you not be so upset when we play a game," the therapist told him. "I wonder if you would listen to the tape with me and see if you can help me figure this out."

Matt was happy to help. They listened to the previous group together. When they got to the part when he overturned the game, they heard him screaming.

> "Who is that?" Matt asked the therapist. He looked confused and surprised.

> "It's you, Matt," she said softly.

"No, it isn't," he informed her. "You must have made a mistake. That isn't me."

Matt was not upset or defensive. He did not remember that part of the group. Beyond knowing that he was upset and had to leave to calm down, he had no meaningful knowledge of his behavior. He was correcting the therapist's impression. He did not recognize that he was the screaming child on the audiotape.

The therapist and Matt listened again to what had happened leading up his tantrum. He remembered those things, and the beginning of his getting upset. For the first time, Matt realized what he sounded like. He heard what others heard. He realized how long he sounded that way. Even when he was removed from the room, he could be heard in the background. Matt was not denying what he knew, in the usual psychological sense. Up until then, he did not know. He had no idea of what he sounded like until that moment. He had no idea of how long his tantrums were, until he heard himself.

Matt did not want to behave that way, although he continued for years to struggle with tantrums, particularly in certain situations, situations that felt overwhelming to him. He still could not always control himself, but he wanted to recognize the beginning of his reaction, when he had not completely lost control, and remove himself. He was often able to do this. As long as he was approached in a supportive and non-punitive manner, he appreciated the people who were trying to help him. This behavior did not take into account the needs of others or his effect on others, but the dynamics of narcissism did not explain it. He was oblivious to his own behavior as well as its effect on others.

Learning from the Parents

When I work with a child in therapy, I schedule regular collateral meetings with the parents, even when they are working with another therapist. Sometimes I see a child in dyadic sessions with a parent. As I worked more with Asperger children, I found that parent involvement in the child's session was often on an as-needed basis, to clarify information or a situation. The collateral parent sessions helped us work together for and on behalf of the child. Since our focus is specifically on the child, family members may sometimes see another therapist for individual, couple, or family therapy.

Just as I learned about Asperger's from the children, I also learned a great deal from their parents. Although they were sometimes frustrated or felt overwhelmed by the difficulties they or their child encountered, they often knew their children and how to communicate with them better than anyone else. As we worked together to help their children, they shared with me much of the information I needed in order to understand and be helpful. The collateral work with these parents was generally not based on a traditional parent therapy or parent counseling relationship. When I consulted with these parents, we developed a relationship based on collaboration as we both worked to understand and plan for the child.

I found that many of these children have a parent, or parents, who interpret and facilitate for them. This can look like overinvolvement. It can look like fostering dependence. I believe that facilitation is necessary and helpful for children with Asperger's. The parents themselves may not have realized why they were helping and guiding their children so much. They sometimes wondered if their child was emotionally disturbed, and if they were causing or contributing to their child's difficulties. Parents want to be part of the solution. They may wish they were part of the problem, because that would give them the power to do something different. While some parents have an understanding support system, some have relatives and friends, or know educators, who suggest that the parents are coddling a child who is poorly behaved. They may be told that their child needs more discipline and higher expectations.

A developmental history often reveals that at least one parent recognized differences in the child's development very early. This is often, but not always, the mother. The other parent and the pediatrician may concur that the concerned parent is unnecessarily worried. Over the years, I have had the opportunity to work collaboratively with many pediatricians who care very much about the children and families in their practices. They have explained to me that pediatric training generally recognizes a wide range of normal development, and stresses reassurance for the mother or father's concern. For most new parents, this may be very supportive. For these children, it can result in a parent's feeling very alone. These parents may feel that their concerns are minimized. They may feel that their parenting is the cause of their concerns about their child. This can delay recognition and appropriate understanding, interventions and support services.

D.W. Winnicott was a child psychoanalyst who was first a pediatrician. He had many opportunities to observe the range of mother–child interactions in his practice of pediatrics. In his writings, he described the relationship between the child, the mother, and the outside world. He observed and described the role of the mother's adaptation to the child's needs (Winnicott 1992). His developmental theories were informed by these observations, and he used the term "good enough mother" (today we might say the "good enough parent,") a concept that reflected an understanding of the interplay of the child's needs and the parent's ability to respond well enough to meet those needs (Winnicott 1965).

This concept is very useful in looking at parent–child relationships. It provides a view that enables us to make sense of the Asperger child's relationship to his parents. I found that the parental support and interventions that these parents provided, at a level that would be excessive for neurotypical children, could be the "good enough parenting" that the child required. This parenting often results in more adequate functioning and adaptation in the mainstream than the child could otherwise manage. These children do not understand others. In many situations, they may not notice or even know what is relevant and seems obvious to most people. This often requires direction, interpretation, and facilitation from an understanding adult.

In our work together, I found that I first needed to understand the ways in which the parents were effective. Together we needed to identify what they were doing, and consider how it might be serving the child. Articulating clearly and concretely what they were facilitating gave us conscious knowledge. It helped parents to realize that the ongoing need for information, support, direction and redirection is much greater with these children. It is not an indication that they have not been effective parents. This, in itself, sometimes changed the interventions. Making interventions and communication more conscious, more positive, and more purposeful can make them more effective. It often led to more conscious awareness in the child, as well as in the parents, of what was happening and what was needed. It enabled all of us to articulate the child's perspective. It gave the child the awareness of the existence of more than one perspective. It helped to support a basic value in good parenting: know and accept the child you have for whom he is, and help him to exist in the world as it is. This is difficult enough. It is impossible to help a child to be something that is alien to him.

In more recent years, I often recommend that the parents read a book by Sue Thompson (1997) called *The Source for Nonverbal Learning Disorders*. It includes many descriptions and interventions that are useful with Asperger Syndrome. When parents read this and highlight what is relevant to their child, it clarifies the child's perspective and the adult's helping role. This can assist them to articulate their observations of their child and how they facilitate for the child.

Sue Thompson's book was originally published with the title "I Shouldn't Have to Tell You." We do have to tell those with Asperger Syndrome and Nonverbal Learning Disorders many things that most of us understand without being told. These children respond better, as everyone does, when we give them information and direction without sounding annoyed that they do not already know it. That is not easy, but it is what they need. We have to tell them many times, to draw their attention to or remind them of what is relevant. That means we have to articulate to ourselves what we think is "just understood" before the child can be aware of it. The parents and I often found that articulating exactly what we are doing, and what it means to a child, also gave us the words to use with teachers, friends and family, and others in the child's life.

A diagnosis is important, if it provides the knowledge that helps us to know what to do and if it helps us to get appropriate services. As Asperger Syndrome was more recognized and used as a diagnosis, more literature was published about it. Parents often read the literature to better understand their children, and to educate others in their children's lives. Many had already read Tony Attwood's (1998) book for parents and professionals about Asperger Syndrome and found it very helpful and informative. Parents sometimes find other parents and parent education or support groups. They find support services. They find information and resources on the internet. These parents often share experiences, materials, and resources. They are very happy to have me share these with others. Some have told me to feel free to have others call them. I am a psychotherapist, and preserving the confidentiality of those in my practice is important to me. Some may not feel they need this, perhaps because they do not see themselves as traditional patients, but they are tolerant of my need to preserve confidentiality. They even manage, at times, to find each other without my help.

As I came to understand the clinical presentation of theory of mind and central coherence described in the next section, I shared this with parents. This often helped us to make sense of very specific aspects of their children's behavior. It often helped us to understand what to ask of them and how to communicate with them. It helped us to work together to assist the child to understand his own mind and behavior. We often utilized these concepts in working with the schools.

Parents often work with me on school-related consultation, because school issues are so important in the lives of these children. I am in a consulting role. If I have completed a written assessment report or a written school observation report, I may have developed some specific recommendations. However, once they understand, parents often surprise me by their extensive use of this information. Some write or revise goals or interventions. They may develop or revise a behavior plan. One parent worked on a task force in her district. She developed a formula for a binder that parents could prepare for special education or special needs children who are included in the mainstream, based on what she had learned about her child. This binder would serve as a reference for teachers and aides, substitute teachers and aides, and others interacting with the child. Explanations of these materials, and examples of them, are included in the school consultation section of this book.

2

Theory of Mind, Executive Functioning, and Central Coherence in Asperger Syndrome

After I had been working with Asperger children for many years, I met Linda Lotspeich, MD, the head of the Pervasive Developmental Disorders Clinic and a researcher on autism spectrum disorders in the Child Psychiatry Division of the Department of Psychiatry and Behavioral Sciences at Stanford University. When we met, she had been aware that I included individual treatment in my work with Asperger Syndrome children. She asked me to tell her about my work with them. I described my observations of who these children are, as well as my observations of the process that occurred in my sessions with them. I used specific examples to illustrate the process. She listened, and then said to me, "You are talking about theory of mind. You've read the theory of mind literature."

I had never read about, or even heard about, theory of mind. When I did read about theory of mind and executive functioning, as they relate to Asperger Syndrome and the autism spectrum, I discovered the language that helped me articulate and explain what I had learned in my clinical work with these children and their parents. Now I utilize these concepts consciously and directly in my work.

More recently, Dr Lotspeich and I both were presenters in a Cleo Eulau Center Continuing Education Symposium on Asperger Syndrome. In her presentation (Lotspeich 2001) she described the concept of central coherence. This concept seemed to describe and explain aspects of what I had observed with these children. Learning more about this has helped me to articulate my understanding of the gifts as well as the deficits that we find in those with Asperger's.

As I have shared information about theory of mind, executive functioning, and central coherence with parents and children in my practice, these concepts have made sense of our observations and experience, and enriched our work together. Today, there is more literature about these concepts, at least about theory of mind and executive functioning, as they relate to identifying and understanding cognitive deficits on the autism spectrum. My focus is on understanding the child and relevant therapeutic interventions. The explanations below are not intended to explain or explore these concepts completely. I am providing the information as it has seemed clinically relevant and useful in my work with those with Asperger Syndrome, as well as my work with other family members.

Theory of Mind

A theory of mind is a concept of another person's mind. If we have a theory of mind, we can recognize that another person's belief is based on his experience or knowledge, and not necessarily on what we know to be true. Tests of whether a person has developed the concept of mind have involved identifying whether someone recognizes what another person is likely to believe. Testing for recognition of a false belief can assess a theory of mind. *Introduction to Theory of Mind* by Peter Mitchell (1997) is a good reference for theory of mind and executive functioning studies. The explanation and illustration below are from this book.

The Sally and Ann situation is a test of theory of mind that was developed for a study (Baron-Cohen *et al.* 1985). Sally is a doll who has a basket. Ann, another doll, has a box. Sally puts a marble in her basket and then leaves. After Sally leaves, Ann takes the marble out of the basket and puts it in her box. Soon Sally comes back to look for her marble. Children are asked where Sally will look for the marble. Autistic children and normal children under four years of age say the box, where they know it is, but not where Sally put it before she left. This kind of test works just as well in analogous, real situations that do not require the pretending or imagining that dolls require. Mitchell (1997) utilizes the illustrations in Figure 2.1 for the Sally and Ann situation.

Scene 1

Sally puts her marble in the basket and then leaves.

Scene 2

Ann moves the marble to the box in Sally's absence.

Figure 2.1 Illustrations of the Sally and Ann test of theory of mind (Mitchell 1997, p.76)

Observing children judge where Sally will look for her marble when she returns.

Clinical presentation of a lack of a theory of mind in autism

Researchers have demonstrated that moderate and low functioning autistic people, and some who are higher functioning, do not have a theory of mind.

Clinically we see that, at best, they can memorize some information, some rules, that at times may make it look as if they have a concept of mind. This was clearly illustrated in my clinical sessions with an adolescent boy, Tom.

TOM

I consulted with the family of a moderately functioning autistic boy on and off throughout his life. I saw him to assess his current functioning in order to assist his parents and school with his transition to high school. Tom and I played a board game during one of our sessions.

> "I won once and Paula won once," Tom said to his mother when we returned to the waiting room.
>
> "Does your Mom know what we did?" I asked. He looked confused. I suggested that she might not know what he was talking about, because she does not know what we did.
>
> "Oh, okay," he said, and then he told her the name of the game we played and that we each had won once.

Tom's "Oh, okay" did not mean "Oh, of course, she couldn't know. She didn't see us and we haven't told her." It meant, "Oh, now I know what to do, because you gave me some new information."

The next time I saw Tom, we played a board game again. While we were playing, I asked him this question: "Does your mother know what we are doing right now?" He looked genuinely confused. He guessed, "Yes? No? Yes?" and became somewhat agitated. It was clear that he knew that there was a right answer. He recognized this as a question with a yes or no answer. He wanted to give me the right answer, but just did not know what it was. I was pressuring and confusing him with this kind of question. I was asking something that he could not know.

I tried to help Tom by asking a related question. "Do you know what she is doing now?" I asked. He thought about it for a while, but did not answer. Once again, he looked quite distressed. Then I said, "I cannot see her, so I do not know what she is doing. Can you see her?" I asked. That was an easy "No."

Tom knew he could not see his mother, but he did not know whether she knew what we were doing. That would require his knowing what could be in her mind. It would require knowing that she would have to be told what we were doing, or see what we were doing herself, to know what we were doing. That would require a theory of mind. Tom learned that his Mom and I want him to say what we were playing, before he tells the score. This sounds more appropriate, but it does not mean he has any real understanding of why we want that.

A theory of mind in Asperger Syndrome

I have seen many children with Asperger Syndrome who can understand another person's mind to the extent that they may know what knowledge another person has. They can figure this out based on whether the other person has seen or heard something. They do recognize knowledge based on exposure or lack of exposure to information. They can even identify a false belief based on false information. These children could pass a theory of mind test, such as the one described earlier.

The Asperger children who recognize the mind as something that knows or does not know something seem to understand this in the same way that they know what is on an audio or videotape. They would know what was taped, based on their understanding of whether the recorder was present, and based on whether the recorder was on or off when something happened. In my clinical experience, I often find that those with Asperger Syndrome seem to have a theory of mind as it relates to sensory information. They can be aware of factual information that someone else has. However, they generally do not imagine the other person's feeling or personal experience as it relates to the information. They do not know what someone notices based on its emotional meaning to that person.

An Asperger Syndrome child I see solved the very same Sally and Ann test of theory of mind described earlier. He found it illustrated in a series of drawings in a book his mother had and knew that it was something that autism spectrum people had difficulty doing. "I can figure this out," he said when he saw the test for theory of mind. He and his parents described what happened. He looked at the drawings and the descriptions under them. He thought about them carefully for a while. Then he gave the right answer.

This child solved this problem in the Sally and Ann situation in the same way that he solves logic problems. He is interested in and good at solving logic problems. He figured out what Sally actually did see and what she did not see. He did not identify with her experience. This is a child who is consciously observing his own mind and the minds of other people, and we often talk about his observations. He has described to me, in a very informational manner, how he figures out with the thinking part of his brain what many neurotypical people probably figure out with the feeling part of their brain.

A theory of mind in neurotypical children

Many of us have seen puppet shows and theater productions for young children with situations very similar to that in the Sally and Ann test of theory of mind. One character has removed or hidden something unbeknownst to another character who returns to look for it. In the test, neurotypical children four years old or older know that Sally will look in the wrong place for the marble, because she did not see that Ann moved it. Young children watching puppet shows or theater productions react emotionally to this kind of situation. They identify what the character knows or does not know, and they *identify with* her position. They are upset for her. They feel with a character that does not know where something is, if it has been moved when she was not looking. They sometimes shout out where the object is, to help her. They experience what they imagine is her experience, what they imagine would be their own affective experience, as well as the information.

Projective play

The ability to pass a basic theory of mind test tells us that someone can know another person's knowledge. Much of social and interpersonal communication goes beyond this. It requires an ability to imagine another person's experience and the capacity to identify with it. Often, there is identification with the experience, such as the identification of the neurotypical child watching a play or puppet show as I described above. This identification occurs in projective play.

Projective play tells us so much about the typical child and his affective experience, because children express themselves and their internal world in their play. In play therapy, the child does not have to describe and discuss his issues, feelings, or experiences directly. He can play with the toys in a manner that projects his concerns. Different parts of himself may be projected onto characters or objects in his play. This can occur without his conscious knowledge that he is identifying with the characters or objects. Because of the child's capacity to identify and project, we can respond in the play. When we respond in the metaphor of the play, we are also responding to the child.

Children with Asperger Syndrome do not play projectively. Even if the play looks projective, it is not about the self. This does not mean that they cannot pretend. Pretend, they know very well and can explain clearly to us, means not real. That is a fact. Sometimes these children act out videos or specific characters and scenes they have watched many times, often following the script word for word. Sometimes they act out or perseverate on themes from video games, TV programs or movies. Even when I thought a child with Asperger Syndrome was engaged in projective play, I soon found that I was wrong. The child was not projecting himself and his experience. He was, once again, giving me factual information.

ROBERT

Robert was an eight-year-old child I had seen for some time. He had an excellent memory, easily comprehended logical and concrete material, and was interested in insects and dinosaurs. He had significant difficulty managing internal and external sensory stimuli and could have severe, extended tantrums when overwhelmed. He was often unable to tolerate losing a game, and this could also lead to a tantrum. Robert was receiving occupational therapy for his sensory issues and was in a pragmatic language group that addressed social skills.

Robert and I started a "group" in his therapy sessions with me. The group included several puppets, mostly animals and insects. There were two people puppets, the mother and her friend, who waited to the side during our puppet group. His favorite puppet was a lobster, which he held. He did not speak for the lobster, but he did play himself in the group and spoke to the other puppets. It was my job to speak for all the puppets. Sometimes we had a picnic. He always asked the ant puppet if it was hungry and brought the ant a pretend sandwich. Sometimes we planned a camping trip or other outing.

One day Robert wanted me to bring another friend to our picnic. We chose the bee puppet. We decided that the bee was a friend of the ant puppet. I was to play that part too. Introductions were made. I had the bee puppet say that it was worried, because sometimes it stings people or animals. It did not want to sting any of ant's friends.

"Don't worry, Bee," Robert said. "You won't sting me."

"I won't?" I had the bee ask. "But sometimes I get angry and lose control. I don't want to do that."

"You don't sting when you are angry," Robert said. "You sting when you are afraid. I won't scare you. I know you won't sting me, because you won't be afraid of me."

I was very surprised at what, in the moment, appeared to be the projective nature of Robert's statements. I responded as I might have in projective play.

"Oh, Robert," I had the bee say, "when I sting I seem angry, but I am afraid. You understand how I feel. You know when I get scared."

Then Robert looked directly and intently at the bee. Personal space is not relevant when talking to a puppet, and he put his face quite close to the bee puppet as he spoke to it.

> "Of course I know that, Bee," he said. "I know everything about you."
> "You see, Bee," Robert went on to explain, "*you* are an insect, and *I* am an entomologist!"

I had to smile at myself when Robert said that. I may have been looking for projection in our play, but what I got was information. I should have remembered that Robert was interested in and knew a great deal about insects. He wanted to know everything there was to know about them and was happy to share his information.

Projective psychological testing

Projective psychological testing presents a similar situation for children with Asperger Syndrome. The responses of these children are more likely to be concrete information about the stimulus than true projections of the self. It is important to me that psychologists who are testing the children I see be aware of that. If the percepts and stories these children produce are seen as projective, the child may be seen as disturbed in ways that are not accurate.

Responses to Rorschach cards, for example, can seem very disturbed and worrisome if the testing psychologist is unaware that a child has Asperger Syndrome or that these children's responses do not mean the same thing that they would mean with a neurotypical child. A description of disconnected body parts can be a concrete description of a card on which the part of the blot that looks like a head or a limb is not exactly connected to the part of the blot that looks like the trunk of a body.

A child with Asperger's may understand this test as a problem-solving task. He may know that he is to identify the shapes on the cards in the way that people sometimes identify shapes that clouds in the sky approximate. I know of a child who told a psychologist that he knew what the cards really were, even as he recognized that he was not expected to give this "real answer." "They really are papers with ink spilled on them," he said. He went on to explain that the papers were folded in half and then opened again, revealing the somewhat symmetrical inkblot designs!

Looking at pictures and making up stories can present similar difficulties. These children tend to be very concrete and descriptive, because they are actually describing the pictures they are looking at and not describing themselves. On occasion, the child may try to continue a story from card to card, forcing the story to include concrete details from each picture. While this is concerning with a neurotypical child, it may only reflect a misunderstanding of the directions for a child with Asperger's. These children do not necessarily understand aspects of directions that are unspoken. Those aspects are unspoken because they are apparent to most people without explanation.

Modeling

Often there is a desire to expose Asperger children to "appropriate peer models." Yet, it is also often noted that Asperger children do not seem to learn from modeling. Modeling implies learning from something more than a demonstration. It implies identification with the perceived experience, as well as the behavior, of the model. This identification underlies the modeling or mentoring relationship. Understanding this helps us to see why these children do not learn from models.

Demonstration, however, can be very helpful. Often these children learn better from demonstration than explanation. If the "model" is actually demonstrating how to do something that can be learned factually, then observing the demonstration is often a very helpful way to learn a new skill or concept. Those with Asperger Syndrome can learn to *understand* or *do* something from a demonstration. They cannot learn to *be* a way that is inconsistent with their way of being. They cannot learn to be like someone, if that person's way of being is an enigma to them. It is my experience that these children often know and articulate that they are different. They are relieved to have this be accepted. This does not mean that they should not be with neurotypical children. They should be with them so the children can learn about each other and how to be together. They can learn some things about how to get along with neurotypicals more easily if they are not expected to learn to be like them.

Empathy

It is often said that people with Asperger Syndrome do not have empathy. That statement can be disturbing, because lack of empathy is often associated with such things as lack of caring, lack of attachment, selfishness, and narcissism. It is also associated with sociopathy and even criminal activity. It has been my experience that many of these children often do care about and can have very strong attachments to people who accept them. Empathy requires the understanding of the feelings of another person. Those with

Asperger's often do care, even though they do not understand someone's feelings. Considering that they may not really understand why, it is impressive how much they are willing to do for their parents and for others in their lives.

Empathy does require understanding the mind *and* the experience of another person. This is not really possible for those who treat as information what others respond to affectively and by identification. Empathy also requires awareness of your effect on others. Sometimes children I work with become interested in their own minds and the minds of others. They study our minds and reactions, and that helps them as they cope in our world. However, they also often think that our ways of thinking and behavior are very strange and difficult to comprehend.

Those with Asperger's may not have the empathy that enables one to understand the affective experience of another person. But then, those who are generally empathetic may not be capable of true empathy with those who have Asperger's. Perhaps in that situation, we may have to rely on a cognitive understanding, and whatever their meaning feels like to us. It does not have to mean we are not attached or do not care.

Executive Functioning

Executive functioning is the capacity to control our own attentional focus. It enables one to do or to attend to more than one thing at a time. It enables us to recognize what is relevant and shift our attention. With strong executive functioning, we are not distracted by the irrelevant and can shift our focus to the relevant.

Those with Asperger's often do not recognize the relevance in situations or information that neurotypicals recognize. This may underlie, at least in part, the need for sameness. Those with Asperger Syndrome have difficulty generalizing. Generalizing requires noticing what is most relevant in a situation, then noticing it in another situation. We can generalize if we see two or more situations as essentially similar. This helps us understand why someone might get "stuck" or overwhelmed when something seems very new, rather than similar. It also helps us understand why someone might not notice what others consider important or interesting.

On occasion I talk about aspects of executive functioning directly with a child. At times, I have explained that it is like having "an executive" as part of your brain. This "executive" pays attention while you are also doing other things, knows what is happening around you, and directs your attention. It is the executive part of your mind that can be aware that the therapist has come into the waiting room, even when you are busy reading. The executive knows when someone says your name or talks about something you are interested in, even when you are engaged in an activity or another conversation.

Typical children listen when someone is talking about them. When I am treating neurotypical children I often tell parents that whenever we speak to each other in the waiting room, we are actually speaking to the child. Sometimes the child is more open to "overhearing" what is said than when we speak to him directly. We need to be aware of this, and we can use this knowledge purposefully to be helpful to the child.

Sometimes children with Asperger Syndrome do not listen when the parents and I talk. Chris is a child like that. One day, when I came to the waiting room to get Chris, his mother started sharing information with me that she clearly intended for him to hear also. As she talked, he got up and walked into my office, leaving his mother and me in the waiting room. In a prior session, he and I had been talking about "the executive" in relationship to issues at school. I reminded him of our discussion about the executive, and shared with him that neurotypical children often listen when someone is talking about them. Some Asperger children do listen when we call their attention to the fact that someone is talking about them. This child found it curious that some children would want to learn something by listening to what adults say about them. He thinks if we want him to know something, we should just tell him. He does not care if we talk about him, as long as we do not use his time with me to do our talking.

Relatively poor executive functioning is very important for adults to understand, if they have children or other adults with Asperger in their lives. I often tell them,

> If you want him to know something, tell him. If you want her to do something, tell her. Try to say it without irritation, like it is the most natural thing to be so specific. Say it with the most clear and concrete language possible. It is often useless to expect someone with Asperger's to notice what seems obvious to you. Direction and correction, as long as they are given in a positive way, can be helpful and reassuring.

Joey

Joey is a boy with significant executive functioning issues. Joey never seems aware of anything except the specific thing he is doing or talking about. I have a small drawer full of little individually wrapped hard candies that this child likes to eat. He is completely unaware when he drops wrappers on the floor, but willingly picks them up and throws them away, if I tell him that he has dropped them. Actually, it does not seem accurate to say that Joey drops the wrappers on the floor. He definitely does not throw them on the floor. What happens is more like this. If Joey eats a candy while we are playing or talking, he unwraps it and puts the candy in his mouth. He then goes on with whatever he is doing or talking about. The wrapper, it seems, just goes to the floor by itself.

I want my comments and interventions to increase a child's awareness, not to tell him that he is wrong for behavior that he is completely unaware of. To accomplish this, I try to understand and articulate the child's perspective and his intention. Sometimes that means thinking about what I want to say for quite a while, until I am more clear about how I want to say it.

One day I told Joey that I do not think he intends to put the wrappers on the floor. He does not do it on purpose. It just happens, and he does not notice. He agreed, and he thought the notion of purposely throwing them on the floor was very funny. He did a demonstration of what purposely throwing wrappers on the floor would look like, using very exaggerated motions, and we both laughed.

I then went on to tell Joey that this situation worried me some, because someone who saw him dropping papers could think he was littering on purpose. That person would be wrong, of course, about his motive or intention. However, it would not be wrong for someone to think such a thing, based on what that person saw. I could imagine circumstances in which this might present a problem for him. He seemed to be considering what I said and nodded after a while. Nothing more was said about it, by either of us, at that time.

Some time later, this child opened a candy, put it in his mouth, and the wrapper dropped to the floor. While he continued talking, he bent down, picked it up, and took it over to the wastebasket. I told him that I had noticed that he had picked up the wrapper that he had dropped and took it to the garbage. That was something I had never seen him do before. "I did?" he asked with disbelief. I was surprised to learn that he had no awareness of what he had done. "Well, the executive works by itself without our always being aware of it," I told him. Maybe his executive is "up and running." This child knows the meaning of metaphors and that neurotypicals seem to like them. He furrowed his brow, as he thought about that. "No," he said. "My executive isn't up and running very well yet. I would say that my executive is going sputter, sputter, sputter!"

Joey's parents are also working on making him more conscious. When he does school work at home, he may be upside down on a chair. His arms and legs may be curled around each other and around his body. He sometimes makes incomprehensible, strange noises. On the one hand, he is home where he should be able to make himself comfortable; on the other hand, these are the behaviors that make others uncomfortable and may cause him to be ostracized outside his home. He is not aware of how he affects others. He is not even aware of what he is doing.

Joey's parents and I developed a plan that would address what we felt was the underlying issue, rather than teaching him rules for what most people think of as appropriate. We decided that it was respectful of him and his needs to allow him to behave this way at home with his family, as long as his noises were not disturbing anyone else. The important thing, for now, was that he develop an awareness of what he was doing. This was explained to him. The importance of awareness was undoubtedly more acceptable when it was not coupled with an expectation that he should change. His parents were going to occasionally ask him to describe his physical position.

Joey even agreed to be audiotaped some of the time when he was working on the computer. This was a time when he tended to make a lot of noises that he did not know he was making. Again, Joey and his parents understood and accepted that the purpose of the tape was to make him aware, not to put pressure on him to stop. For this kind of intervention to be effective, everyone involved must accept that the tape is for information. It is a mirror. It is *not* a judge. The intention of this intervention is awareness, not criticism. The child himself often may make a change, at least in public, once he is aware of how he looks or sounds.

Central Coherence

It was Dr Linda Lotspeich of Stanford University (2001), once again, who introduced me to another concept that I now consciously and purposefully consider in my work with children and their parents, as well as with schools. This is the concept of central coherence. Central coherence is the process of constructing a higher meaning from diverse information. With weak central coherence, one focuses on details, without relevance to a central meaning. This concept can help us understand some of the strengths, as well as the deficits, of those on the autism spectrum. A Mindship International presentation by Francesca Happé (1997, pp.4–9) that is available on the internet addresses central coherence, a concept which had been described by Uta Frith

(1989), and addresses its relevance to understanding the mind in autism. I have subsequently recommended the Happé reference to parents and other adults who have often found it to be very useful. Their comments and examples have enriched our work.

Strong central coherence enables one to quickly comprehend and remember the gist of a story or situation. With strong central coherence, one can easily get a sense of the whole and not focus on the details. In attempting to reconstruct a story, tell about a place, or describe a situation at a later time, the details will not all be remembered. Those that are remembered may not be completely accurate, but the global meaning will be understood and the remembered details will be consistent with the global meaning or gist. With very poor central coherence, details are remembered and focused on without relevance to a global meaning. The details are not considered in relation to a central idea. A lack of strong central coherence has been suggested (Happé 1997, pp.6–7) as an explanation of some of the abilities, even savant abilities, of those with autism. Unlike the concepts of theory of mind and executive functioning, as they relate to the autism spectrum, this is not only a focus on deficits. It is not a deficit model. Weaker central coherence can explain a strength that relies on an ability to attend to details. Errors in details are much less likely to occur for those who accurately focus on and remember details and see them as meaningful.

The concept of central coherence explains some of the strengths, but it is also useful in understanding some of the challenges of those with Asperger Syndrome experience. We know that these people have an interest in facts and often a very impressive memory for facts. They remember a lot of information. Despite this, homework is often a challenge for these children. It is useful to examine this from the perspective of central coherence. We can understand that these children generally do not judge certain facts to be more important than others. Therefore, knowing what is relatively more or less important to learn is difficult or impossible. In an area of interest, they want to know every fact, every detail. They may already know more than the teacher expects them to learn, perhaps even more than the teacher knows, about a specific area. Homework, of course, is not necessarily in an area of interest to them. It is understandable that learning new information could be overwhelming, if every detail might be as important as another. They may not know where to begin or where to end.

This concept may also have implications for adaptation to environmental changes. With strong central coherence, the global picture is most important, and generalizing makes adaptation easier, because many situations may be experienced as essentially similar and therefore familiar. If details are very important, an environmental change may be experienced as very different, something that has to be learned anew.

Research on the processing of visual stimuli by Down's Syndrome and Williams Syndrome children (Bihrle *et al.* 1989) provides concrete examples of very strong and very weak central coherence. Although the particular tasks these children are asked to perform are undoubtedly too simple to significantly demonstrate poor central coherence in higher IQ populations, parents and others I work with have found that looking at the examples of this concept in certain retarded children has helped us to understand central coherence better. We could then address how this might apply to a high IQ population. The authors refer to global and local processing. Their research demonstrates clearly that global processing (greater central coherence) and local processing (less central coherence) are unrelated to IQ. Neither reflects greater or less intelligence than the other.

Down's Syndrome and Williams Syndrome are both genetic syndromes that result in mental retardation. The subjects from each syndrome were age and IQ matched. The D of Y's and the arrow of dashes are two of the stimuli they used (Figure 2.2). In one task, the subjects looked at the stimulus for five seconds, waited five seconds, and then were to draw what they had seen. The results are dramatic. The Down's children have very strong central coherence (which the authors call global processing). They drew solid D's and

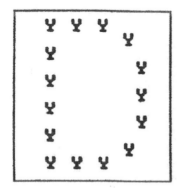
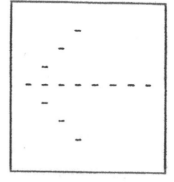

Figure 2.2 Examples of the stimuli
Source: Bihrle et al. 1989, p.42 (© Bellugi 2001)

solid arrows. They did not include any of the details. The Williams children only drew Y's and lines of Y's. They drew dashes and lines of dashes. They did not recognize the D or the arrow at all.

The examples of the normal IQ controls are included. The controls drew what we might expect, a large D made of Y's and an arrow composed of dashes. Their drawings were very much like the stimuli. They included the whole made up of the details. (See Figures 2.3 and 2.4.)

I thought of the situation in this experiment as too simple to illustrate the central coherence concept as it applies to neurotypicals and those with Asperger's. I described the research and discussed an example with parents, only because it so clearly and dramatically demonstrates the concept. There may not be a simple test of central coherence for high IQ Asperger Syndrome children and adults. However, I have come to understand more about this concept and its meaning for them in my clinical work with them.

The mother of a child I see in my practice read the Happé (1997) paper. Anna and her husband had already identified that she had many Asperger features. The paper helped her make sense of an aspect of her own thinking and experiences. She saw that she and her son were similar in that respect. I showed this mom an example from the study described above. I drew the solid D, such as a Down's child would draw, and Y's that did not combine to make a coherent shape, such as a Williams child would draw, to illustrate the concept. I commented, as I drew my version of the stimulus, the D of Y's, that this kind of drawing is probably too easy to reproduce to be effective in discriminating between an Asperger Syndrome and neurotypical person.

Anna appreciated what the demonstration illustrated. However, I noticed that she was particularly interested in my rendition of the stimulus drawing. I had clearly drawn a D of Y's, but she saw immediately that it most likely was only an approximation of the stimulus picture. It was too irregular. I probably did not draw the right number of Y's. My Y's and my D were not symmetrical, in the way the originals probably were. She was absolutely correct. I had not noted the exact number of Y's in the original stimulus. I had never thought of that as important. If I had been asked to copy it while looking at it, I would have understood that the task was to make it as much like the original as possible in that situation. However, I had only looked at it and remembered it as a D of Y's. Even if Anna had seen the original stimulus, and had not remembered the exact number of Y's, she would have felt that the exact number was important. She would not have felt that she had drawn her

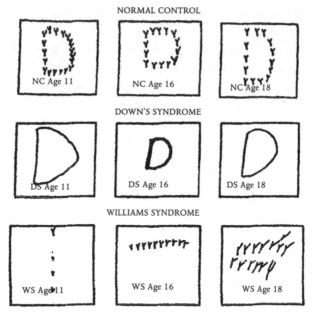

Figure 2.3 Examples of drawings of the D of Y's
Source: Bihrle et al. 1989, p.47

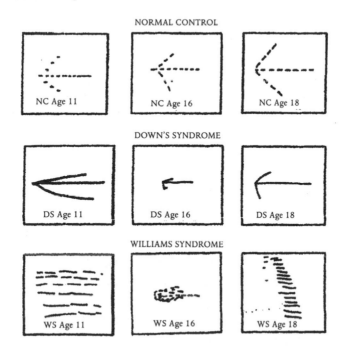

Figure 2.4 Examples of drawings of the arrow of lines
Source: Bihrle et al. 1989, p.47

picture correctly or satisfactorily without the correct number and layout of Y's.

I had a similar conversation with another parent, the father of an Asperger Syndrome boy. While he does not feel that he has Asperger's in the way his son does, he also recognizes that he has features of Asperger's. He had read the Happé paper and understood it. This father told me that he does understand the central concept or main idea, and he also pays attention to the details in his work and areas of interest to him. He said that the whole, without the details, bothers him. He has a profession in which understanding the central concepts with attention to every detail are an asset.

It is common in families of Asperger children that an extended family member or one of the parents has Asperger Syndrome, or at least many Asperger-like features. That parent may be very competent, even very gifted, in his or her areas of expertise. In my clinical practice, as these very competent adults talk about the global concepts and the details in their particular areas of interest and ability, they describe the global concepts *and* the details together. They see them both as essential. They may even see them as inseparable. Several parents said they can recognize the global concept without every detail, but it is disturbing. It is not the same, and they are not satisfied until every detail is present. Global descriptions may seem sloppy, glossing over details that they see as an integral part of the whole.

Attention to the details, as well as the global, is something that many successful people do in their areas of interest or their work. That is not necessarily an indication of poor central coherence. In an area of expertise, it is common to be familiar with and attentive to the details. Many may still be able to comfortably recognize and describe the global, without the details, when that is important.

In my clinical experience, it has seemed that the difficulty, or inability, to separate the global and the details is something that those with Asperger's often experience, when they do understand the global. I have wondered whether this is true of some of those very gifted, high functioning Asperger people who have been so successful in their fields that they have made contributions from which we all have benefited. Perhaps they have difficulty in situations that require recognizing and accepting the global concept without all of the details.

Strong central coherence may explain the ability to generalize. Generalizing requires recognizing what is relevant, the gist, so that the relevant can be recognized in new situations. That recognition of what is relevant in one situation, and then another, makes the second situation similar and familiar, even when the details are not all the same. This is clearly present in those with good executive functioning. With strong central coherence, one does not become distracted or overwhelmed by details that seem less relevant, or even irrelevant, to the central concept.

In the section on executive functioning, I discussed the inability of those with Asperger's to recognize what others see as most relevant. The Asperger children remember many details that most children cannot, and yet often do not see what is apparent as relevant to the neurotypicals. I have discussed central coherence directly with some of the children I see, particularly those who have developed an interest in their own minds and the minds of others. Dan was one of these children.

Dan

Dan and I had worked together for several years. He was an eleven-year-old boy who had developed an interest in people's minds, and studied them. As he developed this interest he was able to pay much more attention in interpersonal situations and even to the teachers at school. Homework, however, was an ongoing challenge, as was keeping track of his assignments. In addition, although he wanted help from adults, he had difficulty accepting directions that would enable him to do less work.

By agreement with the school, Dan's parents could shorten his assignments, and he knew this. They shortened his work by keeping what seemed to be most relevant. To Dan, it seemed that shortening assignments was based on an arbitrary guess and not likely to prepare him for tests. He could not comprehend that his parents could often accurately discern the most important information or what was most relevant to learning a concept. Only knowing *everything* would do that, and there was not enough time to learn everything. Time was even more of an issue for Dan, because he was an excruciatingly slow reader. We eventually realized that he read so slowly, not because he could not read words or sentences faster, but because every word might be important, if he was to understand.

Understanding that there is a concept of central coherence helped Dan. He learned that there were central concepts that were more obvious to some people, but still worried that his parents' idea of this might not be the same as his teacher's. He thought that his parents might be wrong about what his teacher would see as most important. We all agreed, in a meeting at his school, that his parents could shorten his assignments. He was to accept their directions, even if he thought they were wrong. If he followed their recommendations, and they were wrong about what the teacher wanted, his work would be accepted. He would not be penalized for his parents' mistake.

In his middle school social studies class it was relatively easy for Dan to memorize the factual information, once he was comfortable and conscious about attending to the teacher. His teacher presented much of the material in an organized way that was meaningful to him. This particular teacher was trying to give the students opportunities to develop tools that might help them as they learned new material. At one point, she asked the students to skim the chapter first. They were to do this in a relatively short time. She wanted to give them the sense that they could get main ideas quickly, and then learn more about the particulars later.

This way of learning was useless to Dan. He could not skim for meaning. He was very disturbed by what he understood to be a requirement. He thought that reading it his way, slowly reading and remembering every detail, was wrong. It was not really doing the assignment. It might even be a kind of cheating. We needed to discuss this with the teacher, who understood and accepted that skimming was not useful to Dan. He did not recognize the gist. He recognized the details. He had difficulty recognizing what was relevant, even when he learned all of the details. The teacher only wanted him to skim if that could be a useful tool for him to learn. We had to clarify this in order for him to be reassured that he was not failing to do his work the right way. Then he could move on.

When I learned about the concept of central coherence, I told Dan about it. I suggested that understanding this helped me to understand why skimming for the main ideas would not be helpful for him. At a later time, Dan wanted me to explain central coherence again, because he knew that his parents and I had discussed it in a recent meeting. I reminded him that he often remembers details that I cannot recall from a previous conversation, although I recall what I see as most important or the main idea. My memory of some of the details may be inaccurate by Dan's standards of accuracy. Dan knows that he recognizes and remembers details. He does not necessarily think of one detail as being more important than another. He may, or may not, understand what others consider the main idea, even when he knows the details well. He also knows that others do see a main idea, and seem to think that is what is most important. Sometimes he does not really understand the main idea himself. Sometimes he does understand the main idea, but not why I seem to know it without all the details.

I also reminded Dan of the social studies skimming assignment. We talked about it from the perspective of central coherence. For him, reading slowly and carefully enables him to learn. Skimming does not. After Dan and I discussed these concrete situations, I asked him,

"Do you understand what I am saying?"

"Yes," Dan said and paused. He looked directly at me and added, "I understand...but only the details!"

I smiled. I have learned that I should check my perception of a joke with these children. Sometimes I think they are joking when they are giving me factual information not intended to be funny. I asked Dan if he had purposely made that comment about the details because it was what I was talking about. He said he had. I wondered if he said it purposely because he thought it was funny. He knew it was funny, and he thought (probably because of many things we had discussed before) that I would think that it was funny. He was right. I thought it was very funny, and we both laughed.

As I indicated earlier, I have suggested to a number of parents of Asperger children, some of whom have Asperger's themselves, that they might like to read about central coherence in the Happé paper on the internet. At the end of a session, as they were getting ready to leave, one couple told me that they had read the paper. The mother, who is a neurotypical parent, said she recognized the relevance immediately. Her husband, who has Asperger Syndrome, did not see it as all that accurate or helpful.

"People are not born knowing the main idea," he said. "You have to learn all the details first to understand the main idea."

His wife started laughing, and I could not help but smile, when she said to her husband, "That's it! That is an example of exactly what the article is about."

He did not understand. When we talked more about this, I gave him the example of Dan's social studies skimming assignment described earlier in this chapter. With central coherence, one can get the main idea without all the details. Giving him more details, and more specific examples, was helpful. It was still hard for him to imagine the ways that others think and process information. But that is hard for anyone.

I consult with the parents of another Asperger child, more often meeting with the mother. She had read the Happé paper, and provided a beautiful example of the difference between attending to the central meaning and attending to details as memorable and important. The central coherence concept reminded her immediately of something that had happened many years ago, when she and her husband were first dating. He had said that he was going to tell her a story, one that she would never be able to forget. He then told her the story. "I thought I had failed the first date test," she said to me. She knew she would not remember the story he told her. It had a lot of details with no meaning to hold them together. She clearly remembered the event and its meaning to her, but did not remember the story itself. She was sure her husband still remembered it, many years later, and she was right.

When I talked to her husband, he told me that he clearly remembered the story and always will, although he had not thought about it or told it to anyone for many years. He was glad to tell it to me. He and I had not yet discussed the concept of central coherence, and his wife had not talked to him about it, so it surprised me when he said that this was "a demonstration of a coherent story, in that people will link one detail to the next." Then he told me this story:

> A glass, half filled with water, is held up against the ceiling by the end of a broomstick. The broom is at a 45-degree angle between the ceiling where the glass is and the adjacent wall, and it is held up by a rose on the wallpaper. There's a string tied around the rose that stretches across the room. The other end of the string is tied around a crystal doorknob. Outside that door, on the street, stands an elephant, with the end of its trunk around the doorknob. The street is strewn with glass ashtrays. Rolling down the street, smashing the ashtrays as it goes, is a Sherman tank piloted by six red army ants.

He explained to me that the friend who first told him that story encouraged him to visualize the story, rather than memorizing the words. He was to visualize it, and then repeat it immediately from the pictures in his mind. This was enough for him to clearly remember this story ever since. He still remembered it, even though he had not even thought of it or talked about it for many, many years. He sees it as coherent.

During our conversation, he suggested that perhaps he had neglected to have his wife visualize it and then repeat it right away. In his mind, that would have explained her not remembering it. He asked her about that. She remembered clearly that he did tell her those things. She did visualize the story as he told it. She repeated it at the time, but she knew that she would not remember it very long. She did not see this series of visualized images of details as having any coherence. To her it was not a sequence that one could easily remember. It was not a logical progression. There was no central idea or gist to hold the story together in her memory.

This man is a parent with many features of Asperger Syndrome who is very like their child. His wife is a neurotypical woman with strong central coherence. Learning about central coherence has given her a cognitive model that has helped her to understand her son and her husband.

3

Articulating Perspective and Intention in Addressing Theory of Mind and Executive Functioning Issues

Lewis is a boy with Asperger Syndrome who was referred to me by his parents. They had learned that I had experience working with children like him. Lewis was having difficulty attending to and completing work at school. He was overwhelmed by what he saw as annoying or mean behavior of peers. He knew he was not like others, and was pleased when I told him in our first session that I do know others like him. Lewis took me at my word when I told him that my job was to get to know and understand him. The second session he brought me a drawing he had made to illustrate his experience and to help me understand. It is the drawing on the cover of this book.

> "Look at the blue circles," he said. "They are not all the same. Each is a little different from the others. But they are a lot more like each other than like the red circle. The blue circles represent other people. I'm the red circle." Then he said, "Do you see that diagonal line through the blue circles? That line represents their line of vision. It's as though they are all looking at me and are also looking away from me. Both, kind of, at the same time."

I was very moved by that picture. However, I do know that this was not, for him, an attempt to communicate the affective experience of having Asperger's in a neurotypical world. It was information. He was trying to help me understand, cognitively, his perspective of the Asperger child in a neurotypical world. He is pleased to have me show his drawing to others, to help them learn about or understand more about Asperger Syndrome. Lewis has difficulty understanding others, because he does not understand very well

56

how they think and the meaning of their behavior. He has difficulty under-standing pragmatic language, the nonverbal and implied or inferred verbal references in communications.

I often refer children to a language therapist to address the pragmatic language issues that children like Lewis experience. One child told me that everything the language therapist had told him to do was too easy or too hard. This is often the way these children experience school. They think that they understand, they have already mastered the material and do not need to practice, or they do not understand and are frustrated by the assignment. In that case they do not expect that practice will help them to learn. Often, although not always, they are right; learning situations are too easy or too hard for them.

Once, early in their work, the language therapist gave a child something to try that was "too hard." He was so frustrated and overwhelmed that he started sobbing. As he sobbed, his nose started running. "I think you need a break," the therapist said. He stopped crying and said,

"Yes, I do need a break. How did you know that?"

"I read your mind," she responded.

"I want to do that, too," he said. "Teach me how to do that."

So she told him something about how she knew. She told him that she notices sounds and behavior as well as words. His sobs and runny nose told her he was overwhelmed and needed a break. This kind of learning about how minds read other minds was part of their work on pragmatics.

As I described earlier, some of the children I have worked with became interested in studying others' minds. They want to understand how people give nonverbal or implied messages. They try to understand this in an analytical, informational manner. Some of these children have learned the meaning of metaphors. They can use them, at times, to communicate with neurotypicals. The child who told me his "executive" was not running well, it was going "sputter, sputter, sputter!" was conscious that I used a metaphor when I talked about his "executive" working. The layers of meaning we experience in metaphors are not his focus. He uses them as direct translations of information. But it does not seem to matter that his meaning is a more literal translation that applies to a specific thing, and I may generalize my meaning. The communication works, perhaps because it satisfies both of us.

Understanding Intention as We Address Perspective

In my work with Asperger children and other family members, the issue of intention is of primary importance. We address it overtly in examining perspective. It is easy to attribute intention or motivation to another person's behavior. Those with Asperger's are often accused of being purposeful, or of not caring, when their behavior upsets others in their lives. The attribution of intention makes them seem bad or wrong. As I have described earlier, often they do not really understand their effect on others, or even that they have an effect. They may be as confused by what pleases as what angers someone. They are told what is appropriate and inappropriate, and they may be told that they are inappropriate. They are asked to be aware of the meaning of their behavior to others. This amounts to asking them to memorize, remember, and apply rules for behavior that they do not understand. This also means that, to comply and please others, they are often trying to do many things in what, to them, is someone else's meaningless way.

In school, children are expected to be attentive. They are also expected to look attentive, to sit up straight and make good eye contact while they are attentive. A child I know had a behavior plan at school to address this very issue. He was to sit up in his seat, not fidget, and look at the speaker when listening or answering questions. We had talked about what he focuses on when he talks. He concentrates on his thoughts. Looking at the person he is addressing distracts him. He thinks more clearly, and expresses himself better, if he can look into his mind rather than make eye contact. "If I concentrate on everything they want me to do," he told me, "I won't have any concentration left to learn anything."

On the other hand, those with Asperger Syndrome need to live in a world with others. They need to know that they have an effect. This requires knowing more than one perspective. Examining perspective is examining their own mind and that of another. Examining perspective removes judgment and allows recognition of one's own mind and that of another. It allows this recognition of mind on an intellectual level. It does not require that one recognize another's mind by identification or empathic understanding.

The child with the behavior plan and I examined his situation together. We recognized that sustained eye contact was not best for him. To others, however, eye contact means attention and involvement, and lack of eye contact may mean avoidance, anxiety, or even lack of respect. That is not what he means, but that is what others think. We identified this problematic situation. I had a thought, and asked if he might consider whether it made sense to him. I asked him if he knew about "glancing." Glancing regularly can satisfy the other person's need for eye contact, without requiring sustained eye contact. In addition, it also might give him information. When he glanced at the person to whom he was talking, I wondered if he could see, from that person's expression, whether that person understood what he was saying, agreed or disagreed with him, etc. He could understand that and seemed to be considering it. I noticed that he glanced at me more, and I made an effort to be sure my expression gave him information.

Next we addressed his need to fidget. Again, we discussed how moving in certain ways or manipulating objects serves him, but sometimes annoys others. He decided it would be acceptable if he could fidget with his pencil, or some other object, under his desk. This might satisfy him and would not be a distraction to others. We negotiated this arrangement with the school.

Perspective and Central Coherence

From the perspective of neurotypicals, those with Asperger's can seem literal, concrete, and rigid. From the perspective of those with Asperger Syndrome, neurotypicals can be unclear, inexact people who do not say what they mean, and who expect you to know things they never tell you.

Michael and his parents, Brad and Rose

I see a child, Michael, who was formally diagnosed with a Nonverbal Learning Disorder, and whose work with me revolves around communication and theory of mind issues. Michael's father, Brad, is much like his son. He tends to focus on accuracy of detailed information and logical thinking. Michael's mother, Rose, tends to focus on her own and other's affective experience. She thinks about what people might mean, beyond the literal meaning of their words, or what they might feel. There are many situations in which she does not see the central notion as necessarily requiring accurate details.

One day, Brad came in by himself for a parent meeting. We first discussed Michael. Our focus was on understanding Michael's thinking from Michael's perspective, rather than from a perspective of right or wrong. Next, Brad asked if I could help him with something he and his wife had experienced. He needed help understanding her thinking.

Brad and Rose had been traveling in a town they had visited before. They were looking for a particular street. She said that she thought they might have missed a turn by the McDonald's. He had not seen a McDonald's. She said they passed one on a corner a couple of blocks back. He had not seen one. When they drove back, there was a Burger King on the corner. She said, "Oh well, Burger King or McDonald's," and did not seem to see that it was very important that she had given the wrong information.

The issue for Brad was not that Rose had made a mistake, it was that she did not see that giving precise information was always relevant. He could not understand that. He told me he was educated as an engineer, and in his training accuracy was very important. I thought that perhaps he understands accurate information, and logic based on accurate information, very well. Engineering is a very good fit for his mind. Accurate information is essential in his work.

Brad wanted me to help him understand Rose's perspective. He specifically wondered how that kind of thinking could ever be useful, or how anyone could make sense of that kind of communication. How could someone ever think that accurate details were not important? I could imagine a situation in which Rose might have been in his position. She might have thought back to what she had seen and tried to fit that with what was said. She might have thought about what the other person meant and said, "I didn't see a McDonald's, but I saw a Burger King."

Now, I also see this situation from the perspective of central coherence. Rose got the gestalt, and filled in the details. Brad heard an inaccurate detail, and this was so misleading that he would never assume what she might mean. Her assumption helps her in many situations, but her way of thinking would not be helpful, it would be problematic, in a profession that requires accuracy of details. At the time, however, I was not aware of the concept of cognitive coherence. I understood this situation from the perspective of his focus on the information and her focus on what might have been on the other person's mind. It was hard for him to imagine that focusing on what might have been on someone's mind could be a very useful perspective. However, he was trying to understand it and was willing to consider it.

Soon after, this family attended a function in a very large residence in southern California. Michael went off on his own, oblivious to his parent's concern that they did not know where he was. The parents decided to split up and look for him, and then meet at a table to eat. Rose ran into a friend, and they talked about what in the house would interest or attract the child. There was a game room, and they looked for and found him there.

A long while later, Brad came to the table where they were eating, very surprised that Rose had found their child so easily. Brad had worried that something had happened. Perhaps Michael was in a bathroom and could not figure out how to unlock the door. He systematically found and checked the many bathrooms. Brad thought of a possible problem. He logically explored it, attending to what he thought could have been important details. Rose thought about the mind of the child. In this situation, Rose's thought process was more effective.

Both parents agreed that Michael needed to know that he could not just go off and play without letting them know where he was going. He had to tell them where he was when they were out together in a place that was too big for them to easily find him. They all agreed to letting me know about this issue so he and I could talk more about it in our next session.

The next time Michael came to see me, he told me that he had easily agreed to this new "rule" about telling his parents where he was, even in a house, if it was a very big house. However, as I explored this with him, it was clear that he thought of this as one of those parents' rules that he could accept and follow, but he could not really comprehend why they thought it was necessary. He was fine at the party and would not have left the premises without asking. He really was not sure why his parents always wanted him to say where he would be at a party, even if it were in a very large house. In his mind, they had no reason to worry.

I understood that Michael accepted the new rule about telling his parents where he was, when they could not easily see or hear him. The rule is a way to handle this particular situation. I suggested that perhaps his parents wanted something more from him. I waited quietly while he thought about that. After a pause, Michael asked me what else I thought they wanted. "I think they want you to know what might be on their minds," I told him. He looked surprised, and he asked me what I thought was on their minds.

I then told Michael that I thought that his parents had wanted him to think that they might be worrying about him. Parents like to know where their children are, even when the children know that they are safe and are not worrying about their parents. "I wasn't worried about them," he said. I agreed. "I was fine," he said. I agreed. That is exactly why they wanted him to know what might be on their minds. It is because parents worry about where their children are, and what they are doing, even when the children know that they are fine. He thought about that. It was a different way to think about what happened. He was curious.

Michael's mother told me that he talked to her about this in the car as they drove home. He told her that I thought that they wanted him to think about what might be on their minds about him. He wondered if she agreed. She did. Now he thinks that worrying about children is something parents do. Knowing something about his parents' minds can be useful in many circumstances. He may not accurately know what they are thinking or worrying about. Up until then, however, he did not know that this was something to consider.

Perspective and Intention in an Asperger Adult

A woman I see individually, Marcia, has a husband and two children with Asperger Syndrome. I met the couple after their children had been formally diagnosed. My patient's husband, Roger, diagnosed himself after reading Liane Holliday Willey's book *Pretending to be Normal* (1999). This is a book written by a woman whose daughter was diagnosed with Asperger Syndrome. As she learned as much as she could about her daughter, she found that she was reading about herself and her own life experience. Roger found reading this book very helpful. He wanted to share it with Marcia, and actually read the whole book to her. I was touched by that. I also know that it was easier for Roger to read the whole book to Marcia than to summarize it.

Marcia and Roger

The first time I met with Marcia and Roger, they told me about what they call an "Asperger moment" that had recently occurred. The couple had attended a work-related social activity. During dinner Roger began talking about something his wife knew he probably should not share at this function. Marcia signaled him under the table with her foot. He immediately turned to her and asked,

"Why are you kicking me under the table?"

Marcia looked at me and shrugged her shoulders helplessly. Roger made a comment about always saying the wrong thing and not knowing why. I turned to Roger and said,

"I wonder if Marcia has told you that when you don't understand what she has said or done, you should just ask."

"That's right!" he said.

Then I said to Marcia,

> "And I'll guess that you didn't tell Roger that if you are saying or doing something that no one can see or hear but him, it means it's private. If he doesn't understand, he should wait until no one else can hear to ask about it?"

> "No, I didn't," she said shaking her head, smiling, and holding her hands up helplessly.

> Roger said, "Oh, so that's it. That's what that was all about."

Roger runs a successful business that is affiliated with a national organization. He is generally removed from the operations of the larger organization. However, during one period of time he was involved in negotiations with the national group. These talks would potentially have significant consequences for what he was doing in his company. He did not understand the nuances of their negotiations, and the others did not respond as he expected to his communications. He became agitated and depressed. He was not sleeping. Marcia was very worried about Roger, and I gave her the name of a psychiatrist for him to consult. Shortly after that, I had a message from Marcia that Roger still did not have an appointment with the psychiatrist. However, he had agreed to come in to see me during her appointment time later that day. She asked me to please see him instead of her during that time.

Roger came for the appointment. I told him that his wife had said that he was experiencing a lot of stress at work. Would he tell me what was happening? He described what seemed to be a bizarre series of communications, if you took them at face value. He did not know why his associates were behaving as they were. I wondered out loud why they were behaving as they were. What could we imagine that would make sense of it? He did not know how to think about it that way. It seemed possible to me that they assumed he was withholding information or being manipulative. He was not, he said. I understood that he was not. That was what he knew, but might not be what they thought. He knew that he never purposefully withheld information that they needed, to be manipulative or for any other reason. I understood that, and I also understood that they might think that he did. I also wondered if they were implying things that they assumed he understood, things he did not understand or even recognize? If they were, he was not aware of that, he assured me.

As we talked, it became clear to both of us that he might not understand their thinking and they most likely did not understand his. I wondered if they knew that. I found myself attempting to clarify Roger's perspective and recognizing that theirs might not be the same. Perhaps they assumed that he thinks like they do. Perhaps they assumed that there is a hidden agenda in his communication. I clarified some possible differences in their thinking. He seemed to like this explanation of the problem situation. As he got up to leave, he said, "This was not so bad. I didn't think I would know what to talk about when I came."

A week later, I asked my patient how her husband was. She told me that after he and I met, he had a telephone conference with the relevant people with whom he had been communicating. He told her in detail about that conference call. Roger told his associates that he always tells the truth and always means exactly what he says. He never says one thing when he means something else. He will not be doing things differently than the way he says he will do them. There are no hidden meanings or agendas. He told them that he assumes that others mean what they say. If they are implying something that they think he understands, they are wrong. He is only confused by that.

Roger also told his business associates that he wanted them to know that he has Asperger Syndrome. He is very good at his work, but not very good at understanding people's communications. He has always been this way and always will be this way. If they want him to understand something, they have to tell him clearly. His associates must have accepted what he said. Perhaps they had been as confused by him as he was by them. Perhaps this explanation actually helped them make sense of their experience of him. In any case, they were able to work things out and he has continued to be very successful in his business.

Recognizing the very real existence of more than one valid perspective seemed to lead Roger to the decision to explain himself to the others with whom he was communicating. Roger's solution to this problematic communication was not my suggestion. I do not think I ever would have thought of it, and I was very surprised to hear that he had done it. As a psychotherapist, I have often had this experience. People often arrive at ideas and solutions that work much better for them than the ideas that I might have, once we understand and articulate their experience and their situation.

4

The Understanding
and Communication of Information

Theory of mind and central coherence have helped me to understand another Asperger quality. People with Asperger Syndrome often talk on and on about something they are interested in, if they have a willing or at least a tolerant audience or listener. Conversation is difficult. Some tell me that they have learned to be silent, especially in social situations, because they do not think that others want to hear from them. Others have said that they are aware that people may feel that they talk too little or too much. This issue is illustrated very well in a movie, a French comedy, called *The Dinner Game* (1998). The invited guests are socially awkward people who are very concrete and who talk on and on about their special interests. I learned to understand this better from a family who have a boy with Asperger Syndrome.

Jack

Jack is a nine-year-old boy. He is very much like his father, Dave, who believes that he has Asperger Syndrome too. Dave is a competent professional, but has experienced occasional difficulties at work when he understood and acted on communications literally. He once understood a supervisor to be making a suggestion, when the supervisor made this offhanded sarcastic remark, "You better have some expert opinion to back you up, before you make claims like that!" He understood this literally, and took the problem to a number of more senior professionals, who supported his findings. He then presented this at a large meeting. He did not know his supervisor would be surprised.

On another occasion, Dave received a flippant e-mail from within the company, stating that they should just ask certain people (outside the

company) a series of questions. The writer then listed a series of oversimpli-
fied, sarcastic questions. Dave forwarded the e-mail with the questions to the
outside people. The writer of the original e-mail was very upset. "Couldn't
you see that was not intended to be forwarded?" he asked. "If you want me to
know that," Dave told his colleague, "mark your e-mail 'For Internal Use
Only'!"

I work with Jack individually, consult with the school as needed, and see
his parents regularly. In the collateral parent work, we have agreed that Jack's
mother, Elizabeth, is generally translator and facilitator. Jack's father is our
consultant who helps us understand his and the child's mind.

Dave, Elizabeth and I attended a school meeting regarding their son. The
school speech therapist discussed Jack's difficulty in responding appropriately
to a question. She described a situation to Jack in which he and another boy
are walking. He sees a puddle ahead. She asked him what he would say to his
friend. Jack gave a long response that included "You'll get wet. Your Mom
might be mad. Stop. Don't step in the puddle. You might have to change your
clothes." An appropriate answer was included with a lot of additional
comments that were not necessary or relevant.

Dave said he was very familiar with this kind of scenario. The problem, he
said, was that Jack did not know what information or how much information
to give. In his work, Dave told us, there is a concept called the "stopping rule."
The child does not know the "stopping rule." Dave went on to say that he
could imagine Jack saying even more things, such as, "There will be more
laundry. The wash will have to be done sooner. The clothes will wear out
sooner."

I knew that Jack's father faces this situation often, as he tries to figure out
how much to say to people. The next time we met, I asked him to tell me more
about the "stopping rule." He told me that this is a concept used in solving
specific problems in his work. I then asked the parents how we know the
"stopping rule" in conversation. Elizabeth said, "How do we?" with an
expression and tone that communicated that she does not know how she
knows it, but she does know the "stopping rule." She knows how much to
communicate or what the questioner wants to know.

Dave did not know how most people know when to stop giving information in conversation. I suggested that we think about the mind of the other
person, rather than only thinking about the subject matter at hand. The child
responded as if the question asked for information about the subject of
stepping in puddles and getting wet. Actually, to answer this question

required considering the mind of the other (lack of awareness of the puddle ahead). The response needed to address what the other person needed to know. Then saying, "Careful. There's a puddle ahead" is sufficient. Conversation requires awareness of the mind of the other. What does the other person need or want to know? "Oh, is that what that's about?" Dave said. It is often difficult for him to make sense of what most people want to know. He appreciates when we understand his perspective and also address, in a way that he can understand, what others want to know.

Knowing the relationship of the "stopping rule" to the mind of the other is important in conversation. It is also important in understanding school assignments and in work situations.

Jim

Jim is a boy with Asperger Syndrome. In California schools, fourth grade children study California history. Studying the California missions is an important part of studying California history, and often a report or project is required. When Jim was in fourth grade he had to prepare a California mission report. He was very anxious about this report. He was interested in the missions. He had read a lot about them, and his parents had taken him to visit many of them. He had so much to say that he was worried he would not be able to complete the report on time. As the due date approached, Jim expressed more and more anxiety that he would not be able to finish. When the due date passed, I asked him if he had finished his report. He told me that he had not. "What did you do?" I asked. He told me that he had to turn his report in the way it was. The teacher would not give him more time.

I had asked if I could see Jim's report, and when he got the report back, he brought it in. "It's not really finished," he said as he handed it to me. He had gotten an "A+." It was the most complete mission report I have ever seen. I told him that and said that it looked like a very complete report to me.

"No," Jim said. "It's not finished. There's a lot more information that I didn't have time to put in it."

"It seems like the teacher thinks it's finished," I said next.

"Well, she's wrong!" he said.

Clearly, my response did not reflect an understanding of Jim's perspective. I was supposed to understand his position. As I thought about this, I realized that most children accept what the teacher expects as the assignment and try to do what she wants. At that time Jim did not know that. He really did not know how other children wrote less complete reports or why they were acceptable. We explored this together. He understood it cognitively, as a perspective that might exist, but he did not like it. He did not agree with what the teacher thought was an adequate report.

The next year, Jim was in the fifth grade, the year that students study the states that make up the United States. That year he was required to prepare a report about a state. We wanted him to know that there are at least two perspectives on the state report. His parents and I discussed this goal with his teacher at the beginning of the school year. We wanted him to be able to articulate what the teacher wants, and accept that as the assignment which is required of him, even though he does not like it. The teacher only wanted the assigned report, but agreed that he could work on an expanded version in addition. That would be for extra credit. This was hard for him. It is difficult to accept perspective as different from right or wrong. He thought his teacher's idea of a complete report was ridiculous. However, he was able to do what his fifth grade teacher wanted with considerably less anxiety than he had experienced the year before.

It is helpful to understand this situation by considering central coherence. It is difficult for Jim to see that the "whole" can be essentially complete to most people, without all of the details. This can be particularly disturbing in areas of interest. He is able to learn and remember all of the details. To him they are all equally important and essential.

Jim's mother, Sarah, is a lot like him. She has been very successful in her computer industry career. She is very bright, and she is extremely detailed and thorough in all her work. When she and I discussed the central coherence concept, she saw clearly that she and Jim were similar in this regard. That is why it takes her a long time to do things. She does everything very thoroughly.

Jim's mother told me that recently Jim's father, Tom, helped Jim to make a map for a school assignment. She marveled at how quickly they were able to finish it. She was aware of missing details, and would not have been able to leave them out. She knew intellectually that Tom was right, that all the details were not important for this particular map assignment. The teacher would not expect them to spend hours getting every detail correct. Sarah knew that she needed to leave them alone to do it Tom's way, but that was hard and took conscious effort. She also knew she could not have done it that way herself.

Jim's mother is able to see what others think is most relevant, when that is necessary, but it is difficult. She still takes copious notes at meetings. She knows what the central relevance is, but not without thinking it through and considering many details first. In the moment, she cannot easily determine which details are important. She feels much more comfortable looking over her notes later. She then crosses out everything she does not think she needs in order to do her part of the job. Sarah is in an executive position, and is aware that people see that many of her questions address clarification of details. She knows that there is an expectation that she will raise more general questions, and consciously tries to do that. Her real questions, however, are almost always about the details.

We know that people with Asperger Syndrome can focus intently on their particular areas of interest. They can also focus on the topic at hand, if they understand it. Knowing the "short version" requires being able to recognize the gist. It requires understanding what others see as most relevant.

People with Asperger Syndrome may not recognize many things they could easily understand if they knew to attend to them. They often do not know which details are important to attend to. Less central coherence, along with less awareness of the mind of another person, may explain or at least contribute to what we generally recognize as poor executive functioning. They cannot easily direct their attention to what may be important or relevant to others. This is a difficulty that they face. At the same time, it can be a strength to see every part of the whole in areas or subjects of special interest or focus.

Jim's mother sometimes misses what is happening in everyday situations. Her husband shared this example of an executive functioning issue that they both were able to laugh at later:

Sarah had joined Tom and Jim for the second week of a two-week vacation. Twice, before she came, the father and son had a special berry cobbler at a tiny café on a side street in a small town. When the three of them were in the car, Tom turned down that same street.

> Jim said, "We're going to have that berry cobbler," as they drove to the café.
>
> When they went in, the owner greeted Tom with, "You are going to order berry cobbler!"
>
> When they were preparing to leave, the owner turned to Sarah and asked, "Do you think your husband will be back?"

That evening, the three of them were in their hotel room watching television. Sarah turned to Tom with a questioning look. "You've been to that place for berry cobbler before, haven't you?" she asked. We have to know what to pay attention to, in order to know what is going on around us. Hours later, Sarah had finally put together what had happened earlier that day.

5

Addressing Commonly Occurring Issues

The observable behaviors associated with Asperger Syndrome often come up as issues in a child's life, and therefore as issues to understand in our work. I have addressed some of these as they occurred with children in the vignettes I have used. Certain issues come up very frequently in working with these children. It may be useful to examine some that are very common in more detail. As with everything we address, understanding the child's perspective first provides a basis for our work. It may help the child to understand his or her needs, behaviors, and mind. It clarifies that his perspective exists, and makes sense of his perspective. It clarifies the existence of other perspectives and what they may be.

Response Time and Eye Contact

Some people with Asperger's have difficulty maintaining the pace of talking and responding that neurotypicals expect. I have worked with children like this and it can be impossible for me to tell from their expression or demeanor if they have heard and are thinking, or if they have not heard. They may be unaware of this. Some have told me that they notice that others start talking, or change the subject, when they are not finished. They may find that others repeat statements or requests. They have heard, but just have not responded yet. Sometimes they do not see why one would respond with acknowledgment to a comment, if it does not contain a question. If I note my confusion (about whether they have finished, or heard me, or planned to respond soon) a child may give information to help me. The object is to make both of us aware of his process and what it means to him. If a problem arises, we can understand what it might mean to someone else. In our relationship, it becomes clear that my way might be different, but I want to understand and be respectful of the child's way.

Poor eye contact is a common issue described by neurotypicals as we communicate with Asperger children and adults. This is because neurotypicals utilize eye contact to regulate social interaction. We make assumptions about poor eye contact. We may assume that it means such things as shyness, poor self-esteem, disinterest, or even disrespect. Children can be trained, or train themselves, to have more eye contact. As they get older, they may get more comfortable with this. They learn to have eye contact because they have learned that it is expected by others.

In discussing eye contact with a child, I assume that there is a reason why someone does not make very much eye contact when we are talking. It is more comfortable and, in some way, easier. Eye contact is not usually taught. It occurs because it is useful. Could it not be useful, to someone who does not use it? Could it be worse than that? Could it actually interfere in some way?

Many children with Asperger Syndrome can tell me why others want them to have eye contact. They do this easily, but not because they understand others' use of eye contact. They tell me what they have heard many times. Eye contact means you are paying attention to the person who is listening to you. It means you are paying attention when the other person is talking. It is respectful, and not looking at someone you are talking to is disrespectful. That is why others ask for eye contact, perhaps. In discussing eye contact, it is generally apparent that these children expect to be criticized or corrected.

Every child does not have the same reason for not making eye contact. Understanding a child's perspective as valid requires knowing what an experience is for a particular child. If a child is willing, we can explore his or her lack of eye contact. It helps if I tell the child that I have talked about this with others like himself. I have always found that there is a good reason for what these children do, a reason that makes sense for them. I want to understand the reason so I can understand them. As with other things, I need their help to do that.

Stephanie

Stephanie was a young teen who rarely made eye contact when she talked to others or responded to questions and comments. When I raised this issue with her, she acknowledged that eye contact was uncomfortable for her, but did not know why. When people directed her to make more eye contact, she did not want to talk to them. She wanted to get away. She knew that poor eye contact was considered disrespectful.

> "I do know that some people think it is disrespectful if you don't look at them when you talk to them," I said.

> Then I asked, "Are you trying to be disrespectful?"

> "No," Stephanie answered.

> "I didn't think so," I went on. "I thought you were trying to be comfortable."

> "That's right," she said.

In an earlier section I referred to a child who looks in his mind when he talks. It was difficult for him to look at the other person and think at the same time. I told Stephanie that I knew why some Asperger children do not make much eye contact, and shared what that boy had told me as one possibility. I asked if that was true for her. She thought about this. She does look in her mind a lot, but that was not the reason. She is not distracted by what she sees in her mind, she told me. It is something else. It is too hard to look. That is as far as we could go at that time. For the time being we did not know a possible reason why it was hard.

Sometime later, Stephanie was examining and lining up some knick-knacks as we sat and talked intermittently. She rarely looked up. In the course of our talking, I noticed that I had made a statement in a questioning tone. She responded as though it was a question. This is something neurotypicals do all the time in conversation. Sometimes those with Asperger's respond to the content without taking the tone into account. In thinking about it, I realized that Stephanie did recognize the request for a response from the tone, and could be more responsive than children with much better eye contact sometimes were.

> "I noticed that I made a statement with a questioning tone, and you knew I meant it as a question and answered," I told her. "I said that you did not want to go on the field trip, but you knew I was asking if that was true just from my tone."

> "I do that a lot." Stephanie was obviously pleased that I noticed.

> "So looking is hard, but listening is not?" I said.

> "That's it," Stephanie said.

It was clear, as she talked more about this, that Stephanie could think about what she heard, but was overwhelmed by what she saw. The stimulus was too much to process. She could picture things easily from auditory information. That, too, could be overwhelming when the information was graphic and gross (such as some comments the boys made at school). However, sound was generally easier for this particular child to deal with than complex visual stimuli such as facial expressions. Other visual stimuli could be overwhelming also, and she tried to avoid them.

We first identified the dilemma created by Stephanie's needs and the expectations of others. After that was clear, we explored glancing as a tool that satisfies others (those who think not looking is disrespectful). I also wondered if glancing might give her a little information that might not be over-whelming, perhaps if the glance was very brief. I mentioned this as something she might think about. Perhaps she will have some other ideas and share them with me. For now, we settled for understanding both perspectives.

Mannerisms and Repetitive Behaviors

Although some children with Asperger Syndrome look and act like most neurotypical children, others engage in self-stimulating activities. They may twirl or fidget with objects, flap their fingers or hands, pull or twist their hair. They may mouth or chew on objects, their clothes, or their fingers. They may rock or bounce. These behaviors or habits may be more acceptable for young children. Preschool and kindergarten peers often accept a wide range of behavior from others without comment. Occupational therapy interventions and school plans can reflect recommendations for acceptable ways that children can meet their needs to engage in these behaviors. While these activities may make others uncomfortable, they may actually be soothing and may even help these children to stay focused. At the very least, these activities help them to stay calmer. Tolerating these behaviors requires our under-standing that the need is appropriate, even if the behavior is not socially acceptable.

As children get older, these behaviors are more disturbing to others and there is an expectation that the child will learn to control them. The child may learn to see these behaviors as bad habits that disturb others. Children have told me that they wish they could get rid of these bad habits. In our work, I try to identify and articulate the child's perspective regarding these habits. They have an opportunity to think about this and correct my perceptions. Again, I assume that the child does these things for an important reason. They are problematic, because he lives in a world in which most people do not do these things and see them as inappropriate or disturbed.

Aaron

Aaron was a very bright, high functioning eleven-year-old Asperger child. He was much more rigid than his neurotypical parents and brothers, only liked predictable and structured activities, but was functioning very well in a mainstream environment. When Aaron came to see me, he told me about problems or frustrations in his life, his opinions and thoughts about what was right or wrong, and we played board games. The only easily identifiable self-stimulating behavior he had was shaking his hand in his peripheral vision when he was overstimulated. He was embarrassed by this, but I thought we had to find out why it was important and acceptable first. I suspected that he was embarrassed because he thought his need to do it was wrong or weird. One day Aaron and I were playing The Ungame (described earlier). He got a "Tell it like it is" card that asked what he wanted to change about himself.

"I want to get rid of my bad habit," he said, demonstrating.

"Why do you want to get rid of it?" I asked.

"Because it is a bad habit," he replied.

"Hmm," I said, "I thought you did that because it feels good to you. I thought maybe you wished that everyone would think it is a fine thing to do. Then you could do that whenever it feels like a good thing to do."

"That's true," he said.

"I thought you might wish that you could do that with your hand and have everyone understand that it is relaxing," I continued. "Maybe you want to get rid of it because most people don't do it."

"It would be easier if everyone did it," he said.

Often, with this approach, children tell me that they wish that their habits were perfectly okay with everyone else. They only wish that they did not have the habit because others disapprove or think that they are weird. It seems to me that they do these things because it helps them. The problem is that others are bothered, so they do not want to have others see them.

Children like this view, probably because it reflects their perspective as well as their experience with others. Several older children I have worked with have told me, or their parents have told me, that they often go to their rooms to do these behaviors after school, when no one can see them. It is very reassuring to them when I understand and accept their need and also confirm the effect they have on others and the need to consider that. This supports a sense that it is acceptable for them to be who they are. It supports their awareness and acceptance of what will be expected by those who are not like them.

Understanding the meaning of a habit or behavior to a specific Asperger child is especially important when the behavior seems to indicate a specific diagnosis and treatment intervention. Stephanie, described earlier, pulled her hair out, one hair at a time.

Stephanie

Stephanie appeared to meet the diagnostic criteria for Trichotillomania (American Psychiatric Association 1994). Psychotherapy, cognitive interventions, and medications that have been successful in the management of Trichotillomania were not effective. A school observation by a colleague, and my initial clinical work with Stephanie, revealed that her Asperger's provided a much more accurate picture of the meaning of her behavior. Hair pulling, for this child, was a self-soothing activity. Initially, she was not necessarily aware of when she was pulling or if anyone was present or watching. Eventually, so much attention was brought to this behavior that she did become more conscious of when she pulled.

Stephanie was very relieved when I recognized that hair pulling was something that helped her feel more comfortable. It was hard for her that others wanted her to stop. The only negative, to her, was the hair loss. She also liked her long brown hair. She liked her hair better than the wig that she now wore in public. We both understood that she wanted to have her hair and pull it too!

Stephanie knew, of course, that she could not have her hair and also pull it out. After living with this dilemma for quite a while, she decided that she wanted to try to stop pulling. She and her mother agreed that she could have a manicure with long nails, long enough, at least, to make pulling individual hairs much more difficult. She thought that this would help. She and her parents knew that this might only be a temporary solution, but it was helpful for the time being.

Stephanie also remembered that chewing her tongue was very soothing, and she started doing that again. She was aware of the chewing, perhaps because she was consciously substituting this behavior. She decided not to do it at school. There was a rule against chewing gum at school, and people would think that she was chewing gum when she chewed her tongue. Stephanie had braces, and was not allowed to chew gum. We have decided that if she still wants to chew when her braces are taken off, we can ask the school to allow her to chew gum.

Peer Relationships

Often families, schools, and even Asperger children themselves talk about peer issues. As with every other issue, figuring out who the child is and what he or she needs is important. Understanding others and how to function in the larger world is then easier to address in a meaningful way. If we take this perspective with these children, we address them respectfully.

Some Asperger children tell me they want more friends. However, if I question them about the other children they know, they really do not want many of them for friends. They may just assume that making friends is something they are supposed to do, like reading and math. They do often want to do the right thing, as they understand it. Generally, they do not particularly want to be popular. They want to be accepted as they are. When they are accepted, most often by family or family friends, they are pleased.

The most comfortable relationships that these children have, I have found, are with those who share their interests and who accept them as they are. They can learn proper host or guest behavior, and need to learn it. They can also learn the situations in which they can be themselves. It is important that they recognize and differentiate situations in which they must be conscious of someone's needs or proper behavior. They can also be conscious of the situations in which they can hang out with someone who does not mind if they leave the room to play a video game, use the computer, or read in the middle of a visit. Some situations that are positive group activities or recreational group opportunities may work for these children. Understanding these factors helps us plan meaningfully for them. It helps us to accept and validate their subjective experience.

Talking about Asperger Syndrome

Talking to a child about Asperger Syndrome is an issue that sometimes arises during the diagnosis or treatment. The parents or any of the child's therapists or educators can do this. I have had children tell me that they are different from everyone else. They can be relieved to know that they have Asperger's, if this is presented in an accepting and informational way. They may be especially interested in knowing that there are others like them.

The children I work with generally know that they have strengths and abilities that are unusual. They also know that they are not like others, but are interested in knowing that there are others like them. Some children know about Asperger Syndrome, and can sometimes give me a textbook definition. I had explained to one of these children that I have met and know quite a few children like him. Children like him have helped me to learn about how they think and helped me to understand them. It is my job to understand him, I told him. I needed his help to do that. I thought he understood, but I was not so sure when I talked with his parents. On the ride home he had told his mother that I know a lot about Asperger Syndrome. She asked how he knew that, and he said it was because he noticed I had books on my shelf with Asperger in the titles!

Sometimes parents want me to tell their child about Asperger's. When I do, I often ask if the child thinks she is mostly like others or mostly not like others. Sometimes a child has told me he is an alien from another planet where everyone is more like him. Sometimes a child has said there is no one like him, or she does not know anyone like her. In those situations, it is very helpful that I have books on Asperger Syndrome on my bookshelf.

We looked at those books after I told one seven-year-old child, Justin, about his Asperger Syndrome. I told him that even though most people were not like him, lots of people were like him.

> "Do you know why publishers publish books?" I asked Justin, who was convinced most people were a lot like each other and that no one else was like him.
>
> "So people can read them," he answered.
>
> "Yes, that's right," I told him, "and publishers want people to buy their books. They only publish books that people want to read. These books were published because people have Asperger Syndrome or know others with Asperger Syndrome," I explained. "Your parents have some of those books," I told Justin.
>
> "Let's go get my Mom and talk to her," he said.

We went to the waiting room and asked Justin's mother to come to my office. She knew we were going to talk about Asperger's. The parents had asked me to talk to him, and she was anxious about her son's reaction. When we got to my office, Justin asked his mother if she really had books about Asperger's.

> "Yes, I do," she told him.
>
> "How many?" he asked.

"I'm not sure, but I think about six or seven," she said.

"Seven books!" he exclaimed. "Wow! Okay, now you can go back to the waiting room," he then said to her. We had other things to do.

This "label" did not upset Justin. He was relieved by it. It is my experience that children are generally relieved if they think the way they are is an acceptable way to be. They are upset if they think that a label is an accusation. Older children who have had more negative experiences about being different may not be as easily assured. I often ask them if they want to be different, to be like others and not be the way they are, or if they want the way they are to be fine with others. When the question is framed that way, they almost always want to be who they are.

6

Adults and Family Members

In working with adults and couples, it is very easy to misunderstand the meaning of behavior and language when one of the partners has Asperger Syndrome. If a therapist is unaware of Asperger Syndrome, or does not consider it, the therapist may easily ascribe negative intention, lack of caring, or a true narcissistic disorder to the Asperger partner. That perspective can lead the therapist to lose hope for the relationship. It can interfere with the recognition of the attachment of both partners and the positive aspects of the relationship. Recognizing this is very important in individual therapeutic work around a couple's relationship issues.

In the individual treatment of the non-Asperger spouse (generally, but not always, a woman), it is necessary that the therapist recognize the meaning *and* intent of communications and behavior to each. It is important, but not sufficient, to recognize the effect of communication and behavior on each other. It is important, but not sufficient, to explore the meaning of the partner's actions and words, to the patient. When the partner has Asperger Syndrome, clinical work requires an understanding of the intention of what has been said or done. That is an important aspect of understanding the perspective of each of the partners. The commonly described differences in thinking and communication between men and women do not adequately explain the differences in cognitive processing and their meaning for communication when one partner has Asperger Syndrome.

The therapeutic work can include learning about theory of mind and central coherence issues, and exploring the relevance of these to the relationship. This often enables patients to experience their partners and themselves in a different way. They may be disappointed for a while, and exploring those very real feelings is another important part of the clinical work, but they may not be as hurt or angry. Disappointment is very different from feeling demeaned and inadequate. This kind of clinical work makes it easier for some to accept their Asperger partners for who they are, and not feel as attacked or devastated. It is not reasonable, or of much use, to expect someone to be something he or she cannot be. To accept this makes room to appreciate who someone actually is.

On occasion, someone who is aware of her spouse's Asperger's comes for therapy. However, this is often not the case. The patient or spouse may not be aware of Asperger Syndrome at all. In either case, if a therapist understands the cognitive, emotional, and behavioral features of the Asperger partner, the therapist can help the patient understand. Often the patient wants to understand. If a therapist does not see who the Asperger partner is, but only sees who he is not, the therapist may feel that the patient is in a very unhealthy relationship and not appreciate the positive feelings and aspects of the marriage.

I do not think we can really understand why couples are together. Whatever the reasons, they are very important and powerful. This is not something that is explained by logic. It certainly is not necessarily because they are similar, or even communicate in similar ways. What is important is that they do want to be together, or at least they did and want to get back to that feeling. When one has Asperger's it is often enough for the therapeutic work with the non-Asperger patient to address understanding the intentions and perspectives of both. That often leads to a more understanding, facilitating role that is helpful to both. It makes it easier for them to handle their frustrations and feel their loving feelings for each other.

Undoubtedly, I have been more aware of these issues in adult work, because of my work with Asperger children. As I have worked with adults and parents, I have noticed that Asperger's seems to be more common in certain professions, such as in the computer industry, theoretical physics, and neurosurgery. More recently I have found that this has been described in the literature (Wheelwright and Baron-Cohen 2001). I have wondered if the Asperger brain is especially suited to the thinking required in certain fields.

I see a woman who at first came for a consultation about her compulsive, anxious son. She began seeing me for therapy around her own anxiety. Neither she nor her husband had heard of Asperger Syndrome. My patient and her husband had been married for years. They had many issues, and they loved each other.

Alicia

Alicia's husband, Pete, is in one of those professions in which the Asperger brain seems to be an asset. Alicia is a very bright and competent person. She is obsessive and has anxiety about being good and doing what is right. Her husband has always been more than happy to tell her what is right. Pete does not do well with change or transitions. The ability to generalize is based on the ability to recognize what is relevant in a situation and then to notice it in a new situation. That makes the new situation recognizable as something familiar. Pete is not comfortable in new situations. He is rigid in his need for sameness, probably because slight changes make a big difference to him. For him, predictability requires sameness. He needs to have his life as predictable as possible. Although highly intellectually gifted, Pete does not have the central coherence that would enable him to understand the gist of a situation. For him, with the details changed, the situation is not the same. Of course, even a very routine life presents some change. That makes Pete anxious. When he is very anxious, Pete perseverates in a critical or angry manner. For many years, Alicia was afraid of Pete's opinions and reactions. She thought he needed perfection because he was so intelligent. She now knows that Pete has Asperger Syndrome. Understanding what that means is part of our work.

Alicia first consulted me about their son, Steven, who was very anxious. He was compulsive and had difficulty concentrating. I referred Steven for a psychological assessment. When the assessment was completed, I met with both parents to review the report and recommendations. The testing indicated that Steven experienced father figures as threatening. They were dangerous, and he was afraid of them. Mother figures were experienced as supportive and understanding, but unable to offer him any protection in the face of danger. As Alicia read the report, she understood it to mean that Steven experienced his father as frightening. She realized that this was Steven's experience, probably because she herself was afraid of Pete's reactions and Steven knew that. Her struggle with this became an important theme in our work.

Pete seemed genuinely puzzled as he read the report. It was news to him. He did not question its accuracy. He just did not really understand it in the way that a parent sometimes recognizes something he already knows. Pete shook his head pensively, and said of his son's fear, "He thinks that? I don't know why. He shouldn't have to feel that way." He looked genuinely confused and saddened.

After a moment, as he was sitting looking at the report, Pete looked up and commented to me, "Did you notice how the report is written? This psychologist splits his infinitives." He noticed and commented on a detail in the grammar. Pete was not defensive. He was confused as to why his son felt afraid of him. It was not his intention to make Steven afraid, and he seemed sad about it. On the other hand, he had no real awareness of his effect on his son. He also not only noticed the detail of the split infinitive, he commented on it. He had no awareness that many people might see this as defending against or denying his feelings, or as indicating that his son's fears are not more important than the split infinitive.

Alicia was somewhat taken aback by the timing of Pete's split infinitive comment. For him, this comment was not related to how he felt about his son. He was sad that Steven was afraid of him. Pete responded to the report in much the same way that John, described earlier, responded to his teacher's sharing of her child's impaired vision. John was sorry that his teacher's child lost vision, and he thought the medical explanation was cool. I shared a version of that story with Alicia and Pete. Pete saw and accepted that John thought the medical explanation was cool, and was not disturbed by the timing. He could see, in that situation, how it might have been misunderstood, but only for the moment. Once John cleared up what he meant, it was completely understandable. Most of us experience feelings and information as more connected than that.

At one point in our work, Alicia wanted me to see Pete and her together. She wanted to talk to him about her needs and feelings, in the hope that he would understand her experience. I knew that he did not speak her language of feelings. I also thought that if she wanted something specific from Pete, she needed to describe explicitly what it was and exactly what she wanted him to do. He needed her to tell him, because he does not understand other people very well. I asked Alicia if she could be very specific. She said she would try to write down very clearly what she wants. "This needs to read like a list of exact directions," I said.

Alicia wrote a beautiful letter that read like poetry. She wrote warmly about her husband's importance to her and the many things she appreciates about him. She wrote in generalities about her wishes. She said she wanted honesty and openness to deal with realities from the past in the present. She wanted his support for her and the children to be their best selves. Her request for honesty came from her assumption that Pete meant and thought about more than he said. Pete actually told her his thoughts easily. Her request to deal with the realities from the past in the present was a wish for a process between them to deal with the years when she was afraid of him. Alicia read the letter to Pete. He listened calmly and attentively as she spoke.

"That's very nice," Pete said when she finished reading.

"Do you understand what she wants from you?" I asked.

"No," he said.

"Do you know what she is talking about?"

"No."

"But you like her to read it to you?"

"Yes, it sounds very nice."

Pete loves when Alicia talks to him. He likes the sound of her voice. Pete and Alicia love each other very much. They both enjoy music. They share a sense of humor. Pete enjoys plays on words, and they both find things funny that they may, at times, understand in a different way. They are able to have fun together.

I had been talking directly to Alicia about Pete's Asperger's for quite a while. Then, I became aware that Steven's therapist talked to him about his father's Asperger's to help him make sense of his father's interests and behavior. I felt that I needed to tell Pete what we were talking about, especially now that the children were aware of it and discussing it. Alicia asked Pete to see me and I scheduled a session for him.

During that meeting, I told Pete that I had been talking to his wife about him, and his son's therapist had been talking to Steven about the same things. I said that I did not feel comfortable with our talking about him without telling him what we were saying. That is why I asked him to come in to see me. I wanted him to know what we were discussing.

I told Pete that I actually knew quite a few people like him. They usually thought that they were not like most people. I wondered if the way most people reacted and seemed to understand each other's feelings was hard for him to understand. He agreed that it was. I talked with Pete about the aspects of Asperger Syndrome that most applied to him. I said that many people like him are very bright and verbal. They seemed to have the kind of brain that understands things like brain surgery, theoretical physics, or computers in a way that many other, even very bright, people have trouble understanding. They usually have specific interests that they love to learn and talk about. They have an exceptional memory. He nodded after each of my statements. He may have noticed that some of his colleagues are like him, I suggested.

"People like you do not understand people very well," I said. "They find that often people, especially those they care the most about and need the most, react to them with hurt and anger. This is really confusing, because they generally do not mean to hurt people's feelings."

He agreed. I then went on to explain that people like him sometimes tell me that they are often in trouble with people they love, and they do not understand why. It is not because they mean to be hurtful. It is because they do not really understand what will upset other people. With each statement, I checked with him to see if he had that experience. He listened intently and recognized everything I was talking about, often nodding and saying "yes" as I spoke.

What I am talking about has a name, I said, and paused until he responded. He wanted to know the name. "It is Asperger Syndrome," I told him.

"Is that a medical diagnosis?" he asked. I said it was, but for many people I do not necessarily think of it as a disorder. In my experience it is atypical, but another way that some people are. The challenge was to utilize the exceptional strengths and abilities it presents, and also get along in the world with more typical people. People with Asperger Syndrome often rely on others to help them with people. He told me that he relies on Alicia. When he got home, he told Alicia that I think he has Asperger Syndrome.

A short time later Alicia came in for her appointment grinning and eager to tell me something. Pete had been at a professional meeting. When he came home he told Alicia about his conversation with a colleague they both have known for a long time. At the end of the meeting, Pete's colleague wanted to talk to him. Pete told the other man that he had to go home because he did not want to be in trouble with Alicia. The other man said he always gets in trouble at home, too. He does not know why.

"My wife's therapist thinks I have Asperger's," Pete said.

"Is that a syndrome?" His friend asked. "What is it?"

Pete described what I had told him about Asperger's.

"Well, I have that, too," his friend said.

Interestingly, Pete never looked for information about Asperger Syndrome himself. He relies on Alicia for that. She wants him to understand or at least be aware of his Asperger's, as a frame for also letting him know how he is affecting someone else. Often he accepts that. On occasion, when he is angry and critical, he says what he thinks is right, says that others are wrong and that he does not have Asperger Syndrome. "Have it your way," she once said calmly, with a warm smile, "but either you have Asperger's, or you are a really bad person." Pete took this well. He just does not want Alicia to be angry with him.

Most of the time, Alicia is no longer afraid of Pete. She generally appreciates what guiding him and giving him directions means. She knows that in many areas he needs and wants her to guide him. Generally, that is not hard for her to do. They both see that it makes him much more comfortable and less anxious. She tells him very specifically what he is doing well with people, especially with the children. She tries to notice when he is anxious and wants to be critical, but is trying to control himself.

Pete often sees things that he does not understand, and does not do himself, as a waste of time. This includes some of the children's activities, such as spending time visiting with friends, sleeping in past eight o'clock in the morning on the weekend and then hanging around doing nothing for a while, or going to the movies. These activities actually make Pete anxious and he tries to avoid them. Alicia now often recognizes his critical comments as driven by anxiety. She tells him what he needs to accept, what he needs to do, and she tells him when he is doing well, which is very important to him. He wants to be seen as a good husband and father. He can *do* some things differently, as long as he does not have to *be* someone different.

When Alicia is anxious and talks to Pete about her worries, Pete states emphatically the "right" thing to do or feel. He does not know how to allow people their anxiety and offer emotional support without a solution or criticism. The more anxious he gets, the more critical, angry, and scary he sounds. She is disappointed in both of them when this happens. She may be angry with him, or feel hurt, but she is not nearly as afraid of him. If she remembers, she may tell him that what she needs is for him to hug her and tell her that she will be fine. He immediately responds to this kind of request, and is happy he has done the right thing. Even when she does not remember to tell him what to do, she never allows him to frighten or demean the children.

7

Challenges for the Therapist

A Few More Thoughts

It is easy to focus on many of the ways that my work with Asperger Syndrome is different from psychotherapy with neurotypical children and adults. The focus on perspective is much more than a focus on the individual's experience, when working with those whose theory of mind is based on logical knowledge, not based on identification with affective experiences. Learning that another perspective and another experience exists for another person is the first important step for them to understand others' reactions.

Anyone may cause harm unintentionally. We all have to deal with the consequences of our acts, whatever our intentions were (or were not). However, it is important to understand a person's intentions if we are to understand that person. For many with Asperger Syndrome or Nonverbal Learning Disorders, the attribution of intention assumes a motivation that often does not exist. It is much easier to deal with the misunderstandings that occur for these people if we are first clear about what they did or did not intend. They can learn that their behavior may mean something else to someone else, and accept this more easily, if the focus is awareness, not judgment.

In focusing on the differences in this work, I do not want to forget a basic similarity in the therapeutic work. For the therapist, the similarity in the therapeutic work is this: It is our job to understand the person we are with. We need to do this, whether or not he or she fits our usual way of understanding others. We need to express our understanding in a way that makes sense to our patients, because it is consistent with their experience of themselves and helps us both to know them better. This is what we hope to do in our work with everyone we see.

There is another similarity in the therapeutic work. It is the monitoring and use of our own reactions or countertransference. Those with Asperger Syndrome frequently experience others as wanting them to be different. When I am taken aback by a comment or behavior, when I feel that my own reaction is a need for someone to act different or even to be different, I want to observe and explore this. I need to wait until I am able to consider and to understand my patient's perspective first. Let us consider a few examples of my experience with this in my work with Asperger Syndrome.

Is it Arrogance?

It is generally a positive thing to be self-assured, to be confident. Yet when they are, those with Asperger Syndrome can be experienced and labeled as arrogant. They are sometimes described as arrogant in work, learning, or social situations, much as they are sometimes described as odd. Arrogance is a feeling of superiority or an offensive exhibition of superiority. Those with Asperger Syndrome are generally unaware that they sound superior to others as they give information or their opinions. A pedantic or lecturing tone contributes to this impression. They often do not recognize others' impressions or reactions, and therefore generally do not take them into account. They may not intend it, but I also know that their tone as they explain something, and their lack of awareness of our response as we listen, can seem superior and critical.

When that situation occurs with someone in my practice, I try to recognize and monitor my own response. I am much more effective in examining our communication if I wait until I can honestly see that person's interest and joy in sharing what he or she knows, along with my awareness of why the listener can easily feel put down or talked down to. When I wait until I truly can explore both perspectives, without judgment, we can both more easily discuss it.

A boy that I see knew how to play a mathematical game that I had never played. He understood the game and was happy to show me how to play. As I practiced and made mistakes, he corrected me in a way that sounded amused and superior. My initial response was discomfort. After a while, I clarified with him what he thought about his teaching and how I was doing. He said that my mistakes might be a bit amusing, but he enjoyed showing me how to play and thought that I was learning it easily. He thought I would play very well with a little practice. I told him that I was aware that people often thought that those with Asperger's were arrogant, because of the tone they used when they explained. It was the tone that he sometimes used. I saw that he was clearly dumbfounded that anyone could assume from his tone and his words that he was arrogant. He laughed at that notion, in what could also be mistaken for an arrogant response. He saw it as odd, but interesting, that it is not unusual for neurotypicals to experience some people with Asperger's as arrogant. He knew he was not, of course, but he was very open to exploring what it might mean to someone else, as strange as that seemed to him.

Feeling Hurt and the Attribution of Intention

The same process can occur with comments that may feel hurtful or uncaring. The motivation to hurt or a lack of caring may be attributed to the comments or actions of someone with Asperger Syndrome. Those comments are then judged to be inappropriate, to be wrong or bad in a basic way. When Alicia's husband Pete was accused of being hurtful or uncaring by his wife or children, he became defensive. He accused them of being much too sensitive. Their reaction was wrong, he told them, and they were too thin skinned. When we recognized that hurting someone's feelings was not his intention, Pete did not feel accused. Then he could much more easily accept, as information, that the other person felt hurt. Feeling hurt, even when the hurt was not intended, could also be a valid and understandable response. However, that did not always make it easier to get through these difficult communications as they were happening.

It is hard to separate intention from the effect of a comment or behavior. With time, it gets easier to clear up a miscommunication. With time, it gets easier to not have a strong affective response. When I have an affective response to a comment or comments, waiting until I understand has been helpful, as it is with all countertransference reactions. This has become easier with time and experience, but understanding what has happened and planning my response can still require an intensity of effort, of concentration and thought. For these patients, who are so cognitive themselves, I must also think very hard.

Choices

When adults look at a child's action or inaction, when we describe a child's behavior, we tend to talk about choices. Children and adults are urged to think about choices, to consider their options, and to make good choices. Educators often talk to children about the choices they make. Children are often described as making bad choices when they have problems in school. Asperger children may be told that they are choosing to not focus on their work. They may be described as choosing to call out answers, choosing to interrupt and not wait their turns, choosing to play with objects or put them in their mouths.

We all certainly have some choices about what we do. All children sometimes do something wrong, or avoid something required. It is hoped that they have the judgment to make safe choices about when to do this avoidance or misbehavior. A certain level of awareness of behavior and consequences is needed to have this kind of judgment.

Children with Asperger's may make choices to refuse to do something. They may choose to do something that they are not supposed to do. Often those with Asperger's do not have awareness of themselves and the reactions of others to them. They may not have the same comprehension of a situation or expectation that a neurotypical often has. At those times, describing their situation as a choice is not meaningful to them, and therefore not particularly useful. Of course, they are still faced with the consequences of what they have done or not done. Whether or not we choose our behavior, we have to deal with the consequences of what we have done. To call something a choice is not very useful, unless it was a choice. Calling an action or inaction a choice, when it is not done by choice, is blaming. It is attributing intention when there was no intention.

Choices only exist in a real way when we are aware of them. It helps to know our own and others' perspectives, that they exist and what they are. This may even sometimes result in an additional awareness, the awareness of the existence of choices, of alternative ways to handle a situation, a need, or a communication. At the very least, it can lead to the awareness of the opportunity to actively participate in a process of understanding what occurred or what is being asked.

Spontaneity or Impulsivity?

Perhaps the most poignant situation for me is around the issue of spontaneity. Working with these people has forced me to examine what I experience as spontaneity, and what I experience as impulsivity or disinhibition. When I see a neurotypical child who is depressed, I am encouraged and relieved when the depression lifts. Often that child will then become much more spontaneous. I worked with a young child who was depressed for months. She was always somber and moved slowly. When she felt better, she became much more active. I saw a child who was not carrying the weight of the world on her shoulders, and I experienced a sense of relief. She was relieved herself, and skipped across the room. Her parents told me she had generally been active and could be joyful. They told me that they felt as if they had their child back. I had not known her this way, but this was the child they had before her depression.

When a child with Asperger Syndrome becomes more spontaneous, he may do or say something that seems odd or disinhibited. Like all of us, he does not closely monitor his behavior as he relaxes and becomes less depressed or anxious. As a child becomes more comfortable and accepted by me, he is likely to become less conscious of his behavior. I must then face the fact that as his behavior becomes more spontaneous, it may also make me anxious. His "inappropriate" behavior or comments seem "impulsive." Then I have to wonder – if I do not like this less constricted, more relaxed, behavior do I then call it impulsive or disinhibited? If I do like it, do I call it spontaneous?

It is no wonder that so many with cognitive and social communication issues avoid social situations. It requires an enormous effort to be conscious of their behavior. And even then, they meet with only limited success. I find that they do not avoid other people when they are with people who like them, when they are with those who can accept their natural ways more easily.

Knowing the person we are seeing, and monitoring our reactions, are the usual things we psychotherapists try to do in our work. Doing this work with Asperger Syndrome has led me and continues to lead me to another, very different, understanding of the human mind. It has led me to the interventions with Asperger patients and families that I have described, and it has informed the very important collaborative relationships with other professionals and schools that are described in the following section of this book.

Part Two

Case Management

8

Collaboration with Parents
and Other Professionals

Child psychotherapists collaborate with other professionals who provide other therapies and are part of a child's support system or intervention team. Collaboration with schools is frequently a very important part of child work when children have learning, emotional, or behavioral issues at school. Collaboration and consultation are almost always a case management aspect of clinical work with Asperger Syndrome.

I have discussed the importance of parent collateral sessions to my work with a child. The parents and I collaborate as we address the child's work with other professionals. Open communication supports our roles. It enables the parents to be more aware of their parenting and enables us to consciously plan together for their child. I often address the theory of mind, central coherence, and executive functioning issues that help us understand the child. In doing that, I am generally bringing language and further understanding to something the parents have already observed and are trying to understand and address. As they understand theory of mind and central coherence, the parents (including the more Asperger-like parent) and even the child often bring me examples that reflect their understanding.

The child is aware of my communication with his parents, and often expects it. After all, these are children whose parents often intervene or facilitate for them. Sometimes, we invite a parent into a session so we can understand or figure out something together. At those times, the child experiences the way his parents and I communicate. The child knows that I know quite a few children like him and that I am interested in them. The child and parents generally find that reassuring. Often that makes it easier to address, in our sessions, the issue of perspective and what the various perspectives might be. Collaboration with other professionals becomes a natural extension of this work.

Collaboration with Other Professionals

Our individual work focuses on a relationship with the child that increases his awareness of himself and others. His parents, however, need to help him through the challenges of his life, day in and day out. Often, the direct support of other therapeutic interventions can address an individual child's specific needs. The services and interventions from which these children benefit may include occupational therapy, language therapy, group therapy, and specific educational and/or behavioral therapies. (See Appendix 1 for a further description of my experience with these therapies and interventions.) Some of these services may be provided at school. Often they are provided privately. Psycho-pharmacological interventions may also be helpful. These children often experience anxiety or depression, as they struggle to deal with expectations that do not necessarily match their abilities or their needs.

Child psychotherapists often have occasion to collaborate with another therapist or teacher. Parents, the primary case managers for Asperger children, often learn about and obtain services to help their child. A child may already be receiving other therapy services, or we may refer them.

In addition to reviewing written assessments and reports, telephone contact can support our work and that of another professional. We can communicate our impressions as our work progresses, as well as issues that arise during our work with a child. Sometimes, the initial contacts around the referral are sufficient. Sometimes, more frequent collaboration is needed. Often, I have found, even very infrequent ongoing contact is helpful. Even occasional, brief voicemail messages can maintain a team approach. In addition to making a difference to both of our separate work with the child, this kind of communication is often experienced as supportive to the child and his family. The parents' role can be supported and enhanced by my participation in case management.

On occasion, especially when a child is experiencing difficulty with a particular situation in his life, or with a therapeutic intervention itself, more frequent telephone collaboration or even a meeting is needed. We can at least share our perceptions of the situation, how it presents to each of us, and how we are handling it. Even that may enrich and support the work, as well as support the child and family. At a minimum, we can try to address what is happening from the point of view of the child's experience. Sometimes we come up with a plan that we can share with the child, so he can be an active participant in implementing and evaluating it.

Since the children generally know about these meetings or conversations, I preview them and review them with the child. Sometimes children are not particularly interested. They do not mind that we are talking, but may not see my contact with the other professionals as relevant to them. They may not recognize that they may be affected by my collaborations. They may not expect to understand, and not want to talk much about it. This is more common with younger children.

Sometimes children are pleased and supported by my collaboration with others. They can understand that this is for them. I generally ask in advance what the child wants me to discuss. I also ask if there are some things he wishes we would not talk about. At times we make a list, to organize what I should remember to address. We can talk about the issues on the list afterwards.

On occasion, children are concerned that they were wrong or bad. They may express hopelessness that talking will help. We then have another opportunity to make sure that I understand and can communicate their perspective. Sometimes a child specifically requests that I have someone else tell me the things that are hard for him to explain or talk about. "You tell her," a child may say to his mother.

Generally, however, Asperger children find this kind of discussion, in which I want to prepare to talk to another therapist or educator, to be curious. These children rarely worry about what I say when I talk with someone else about them. The children I know well are comfortable with the collaboration. They may appreciate hearing that it is about helping them or about clearing up a misunderstanding. They are reassured to know that their view of their experience will be addressed as well as what someone else might want of them. For these children, having their perspective and intentions represented and accepted in a positive or nonjudgmental light is most important. Occasionally, an adolescent is aware of a preference that I not share something, but even this is much less common than the usual desire for confidentiality that we expect with neurotypical teenagers.

Earlier in my work with Asperger's I had some conversations with children about collaborative meetings or telephone contacts that I later found very amusing. Later, that is, when I finally figured out what was happening. I intended to be sensitive to the child's feelings and needs. I did not want to compromise our individual therapy relationship by communicating too much with others in his/her life. This concern had little meaning to most of these children.

Situations like the following occurred. As I carefully explored what to do in a way that was sensitive to him, a child was sometimes confused by the intent of my questions and comments. One child understood me to be asking for help in solving my problem of deciding what to do. I had been seeing this boy individually for a while. His family and I were considering a meeting of several professionals working with him, as well as someone from a new school he was to attend in the fall. The purpose of this meeting was to facilitate the school change, and not in response to something the child would recognize more specifically as a current issue or problem. It was going to be most convenient for everyone attending to have the meeting in my office, the very place the child came for his therapy.

I had already realized that using words that refer to thoughts, rather than feelings, made it easier for this child to respond in discussions. I asked for his thoughts and preferences about this meeting. I wanted to know his thoughts about my attending the meeting. He paused, and he looked confused about how to answer me.

> "I don't know what to tell you to do," he finally said to me. "You should do what you want to do."

> "I want to consider what you want," I said to him.

> "You have to make your own decision," he then told me. "I don't think I can help you."

This boy thought that I was having difficulty deciding what to do and was asking him to help me make a decision. I had a problem, it seemed, and I was asking for his help. He did not want to let me down, but he just could not help me with this. I realized that I needed to address this issue differently.

> "I want to have this meeting, if it seems like the others and I can talk about you to help the new school to understand you better. If it seems to you that I can help them to understand you better, that would be a reason that I would decide to go to the meeting," I explained.

> "Oh," he said. This decision did involve his thoughts, after all. He seemed to be thinking it over from this new perspective. "I think you should meet with them," he then told me. "Maybe you can help them understand me."

I also wanted to know how he felt about my holding the meeting in my office. The question about where we would meet was also very strange to him, I soon realized. Neurotypical children might care about something like this. This boy made it very clear that we should meet anywhere we wanted to meet. It did not matter if it was in my office, because it was not during the time of our session. The place we met was not important to him. It was just another odd question that seemed important to me. He knew I meant well, and he was very tolerant of my strange concerns.

Talking about an aspect of my collaboration with the child is very useful in developing his awareness of an issue. We review his concerns and information he wants me to share. I tell him things I plan to say, so we can both figure out if my thoughts seem accurate and if I am explaining them well enough. We figure out together how to understand others or how to help them understand him. In the course of doing that, I need to articulate these things in a nonjudgmental way. I need his help to make sure I understand correctly from his perspective.

I learn, again and again, that these children can understand themselves and communicate, as long as they are not expected to be someone other than who they are. They can learn to manage more effectively in the more neurotypical world around them. It may be difficult and energy consuming to deal with the rest of us, but it does not have to be impossible. In a small way, this exploration of the collaborative process is another bit of what will enable the child to explain himself. He may learn to solve a problem or miscommunication with others more independently, as he gets older and has more experience with this process.

Issues around medication become another area for direct problem solving with the child, as well as collaboration with the prescribing physician. Sometimes children who are helped significantly by medication, and may even be aware of this, do not want to take their medicine any more. The medication issue can be addressed in our work.

Adam

Adam was a child who decided he no longer wanted to take his medication. Even with the medication, which clearly helped, school and homework could be very stressful for him. Learning was not difficult, but responding to all the expectations for compliant behavior and production of work was much more difficult. His parents were very worried about his resistance to taking his medication.

Adam discussed his medication in an appointment with his psychiatrist. He told her that his medicine helped him, but he also made it clear that he did not want to take it any more. She did not want him to be forced to take medicine, but asked him to talk to me about it before they made a change. His psychiatrist had left me a message before I saw him. Adam then told me about this when he came in for his appointment. They both described the same situation. They agreed that the medication helped him stay calmer and less angry. He was less frustrated and able to do better in school and with friends, although these situations continued to present challenges. Despite this, he did not want to take his medicine any more.

This child understood that what he told me did not make sense to me. I needed help to understand. We explored all the reasons he might not like to take medicine that helps him. The pills were not too big. They were not hard to swallow. They did not seem to have bothersome side effects. Although he did not particularly like the idea of taking them every day, that was not the only problem for Adam. He did not like to brush his teeth every day either, but he generally did it because his parents supervised him, and because he and they did not want him to have rotten teeth.

Adam thought very hard to explain so that I could understand. Eventually, he said that the pills made him different. They took away a lot of his anger. Then his behavior was not really his. The pills made him behave better. I asked Adam to tell me who or what was in charge of his anger, and he said, "The pills are, of course." That was why he wanted to stop taking them. If he took the medicine, the medicine was in charge of his anger. If he did not take it, he was in charge of his anger.

This is something that other children have told me. It is not particular to Asperger Syndrome. This situation is particularly common with adolescents, who do not want to accept that they are dependent on medication. Parents may confront this when they have a child with a chronic condition. Sometimes, not taking medications can be very risky or even life threatening, such as with seizure disorders and diabetes. It can be an issue with other conditions in which medications are helpful, but not essential.

I repeated to Adam what I had heard him say. "Other children have tried to explain this to me," I told him, "but I still do not understand it." I shared that I think about this in another way. I tried to maintain a slow and thoughtful discussion of this. I tried to communicate that I was concerned that we did not understand each other's perception of the situation. He had worked very hard to explain his thinking, and I could not understand well enough. Maybe I could explain what I was thinking, and he could help me. He said that we could try.

I told Adam that I thought of medicine the way I think of glasses. I asked him if he sees better when he wears his glasses, or when he does not wear them. He told me he sees better with them. I wear reading glasses around my neck, and put them on to read or play a board game, something he has frequently seen me do. I told him that I can read better with my glasses. I asked him who was in charge of seeing, when he wears his glasses. He said that he was in charge of seeing when he wears them. That way he sees better. I had the same experience, I told him. I think that I am in charge of seeing better when I put on my glasses to read.

I then told Adam that I think about his medicine the way I think about his glasses. "I think of it this way," I explained. "If you take the medicine, you are in charge of your anger. If you do not take it, you are not in charge of your anger. To me, if you do not take the medicine, then your anger is in charge of you."

Adam was very surprised by and interested in my analogy. He told me that he had never thought of it in that way. He wanted to be in charge of his anger. He did not want it to be in charge of him. Then Adam told me to please call his psychiatrist. He wanted me to tell her that he had decided that he would continue to take his medicine. However, he wanted the medicine scientists to find a way for him to take it less frequently. Once a week would be fine for a while, but once a year would be better, he explained. Adam asked me to please tell this to his psychiatrist. He wanted me to ask her to work on developing a once-a-week pill, for now, and then one that was longer acting. He thought this was something that she might be able to work on. Meanwhile, he would take his medicine every day.

Collaborating with the psychiatrist and working with the child facilitated a resolution of this problem. Collaborating with another professional and working with the child does not always result in a resolution of the problem, but it often facilitates understanding and an improvement in the situation.

9

School Collaboration and Consultation

The Child Therapist's Role

For many years, as a child psychotherapist, my work was primarily with children and their parents. The issues of the children I saw did not necessarily include significant difficulties at school. Some, of course, were having problems at school. If a child was experiencing significant learning, emotional, or behavioral issues, I sometimes had contact with a teacher and with other school personnel. Occasionally, I included a school observation as part of my assessment, or arranged for another child therapist to observe a child to better understand the school issues. When the parents and I thought that would be helpful, I attended a meeting at the school. I was available for telephone contact with a teacher, principal, school psychologist or counselor. My role was as a resource for understanding the child developmentally and emotionally. I could be an advocate for the child and a participant in planning, when we felt that it was appropriate and would not be disruptive to my relationship with the child.

As I worked with more Asperger Syndrome children, I found that I became more involved in working with the schools. Even the most capable and high functioning of these children might have difficulty with organization, with understanding expectations, and with homework. Many had interpersonal problems with peers and sometimes with adults. As they got older, they often were frustrated with literature. The language became more abstract. They were expected to understand what is implied, rather than stated. Writing, the decision of what to write or the act of writing it, could be a challenge. Creative writing could be an area of difficulty, if it did not follow a tight structure or learned formula. Early in my work with these children, a parent or the school might initiate contact in response to a crisis or a significant concern. Later, these families and I came to see that I could have a role in planning and collaborating with the school. This could be an important part of my work. On occasion, I primarily consult with a parent or parents about a child rather than primarily seeing the child for regular individual sessions. I may also provide consultation regarding school issues. This latter role, however, has grown out of my understanding of Asperger Syndrome from my experiences with children in individual therapy.

As I learned to understand these children better, I recognized that very detailed school observations could be an important component of and support to my role. The written observation report can then be part of the material for consideration in school planning meetings, as well as in my collaboration with teachers and other school personnel. I have found that these observations enable us to better understand the problematic aspects *and* the successful aspects of the child's school experience. The meaning of the observation and its use seemed to grow naturally from the process of understanding the child in his or her relationship to me. School is a very large part of a child's life, and these children are almost always relieved if I am trying to understand and help.

The parents' role, of course, is always primary in supporting their child at school. Parents handle the day in and day out issues. In supplementing and supporting what they do, I recognize that the most important case management role for the child therapist is often with the school. This might be in direct collaboration, such as with a teacher, resource specialist, or language therapist. Often, it is also as a part of a larger team meeting.

In addressing school functioning, I learned that I need to understand the issues and make recommendations that are useful to and support the parents, the child, and the school. I had learned that I needed to understand the child's experience. To communicate with the child effectively, we needed to develop a process that made sense to both of us. To communicate effectively with a school, and support the parents and child, I must also articulate my perceptions and recommendations in a way that makes sense to all of us.

As therapists, we are concerned about developing an understanding of what underlies a child's thinking and functioning. I have the same concern about understanding the child's experience at school. I prefer to have school goals that address the most basic issues that affect the child's learning and relationships. However, I know that it is not effective to address these issues without attention to the child's observable behavior in the classroom. Teachers must instruct and manage a classroom of children. To communicate in a meaningful way, I have to see what they see and what concerns them, and they must know that. My observations must be consistent with theirs. Then there is a sense that we are talking about the same child. Otherwise, they may think that my understanding of the child is wrong, or they may feel that it is not relevant in a classroom. They might find my understanding of the child interesting in an academic or abstract sense, but not useful to them. My recommendations may not resonate with their experience of the child or their goals for the child. This is true for other school personnel including language therapists and special education teachers.

When the school and I begin with shared observations, these observations can then lead, in a meaningful way, to impressions and concrete recommendations that people can understand and follow. If I address theory of mind, central coherence, and executive functioning, I must do this using plain language that relates to observable behavior. If we agree on what we see, it is much easier to address the implications for this particular child. This leads more naturally to accepting goals and interventions that are helpful to the child and acceptable to the school.

I cannot emphasize enough that in our role as the child's advocate at school, it is not enough that we understand the child's Asperger Syndrome. That is only useful if we communicate clearly and in a way that seems relevant to the child and adults. I try to state or write recommendations that are clear enough to make sense to the child as well as to the adults. Often a few, clearly stated recommendations for goals and for intervention strategies are enough. The implementation must be relatively easy to accomplish. Recommendations should make it easier, not more complicated, for the child and teacher to be successful.

I have found that I often need to clarify, specifically, the need for ongoing interventions and supports. If something is working effectively, that may be a sign of the success of the intervention, as long as it is being used. It seems to be a human tendency – perhaps all of us do this at times – to decide that if something is working it is no longer needed. Many times, I have observed that as we explore a breakdown in a child's school functioning we find that the supportive interventions were withdrawn. The child was doing better, but only because the interventions were in place. Most children let us know when they no longer need a supportive intervention to function well. I try to attend to this issue as I participate in planning goals and interventions at schools with individual teachers or therapists, either informally or in formal meetings. The larger goal that we all have is always that the school experience be reasonably successful for the child, and that the child learns. Children spend a lot of time in school. That time is often much more stressful for these children. At a minimum, the school day should be manageable most of the time for the child, the parents, and the school. This means providing appropriate support as long as it is needed.

Education Alternatives

Sometimes the public school provides the best or only alternative for a child's education. Sometimes parents find a private school that is a good match for their child's needs. The private school may be willing to work with the child's needs and appreciate his or her strengths. An outside therapist can still provide observations, consult with teachers, and attend meetings with school personnel to support the child. Any of the school consultation issues described can be modified to be an appropriate support for a child's private school placement.

Sometimes parents decide to home-school a child. Several parents with whom I have consulted have done that during an especially difficult time for their child. In that case, the individual therapy and adjunct therapies (language, occupational, group therapy) become part of the child's home-school plan. Wherever the schooling takes place, it is most important to develop a plan that supports the child's education academically, as well as his understanding himself and others, and supports his competence in dealing with other people and life issues.

The School Observation

The easiest way to approach school issues from a point of shared observations, a shared understanding that we are talking about the same child, is with a formal school observation. In recent years, when I begin with a new child, I often consider doing a school observation as a part of my initial assessment. This is the only opportunity that I will have to observe the child without his or her having already met me. I have, on occasion, visited a child's class to observe after I met the child. However, I generally have someone else do the observation if I have been working with a child on an ongoing basis.

Many professionals, including psychotherapists, school psychologists, language and occupational therapists, and educational specialists may do a classroom and playground observation. They may use these observations to determine what further assessment they will do. They may use these observations to inform their identification of issues, impressions, and recommenda-tions. I have often used observations in this way. However, my *primary purpose* in completing and reporting on a school observation of an Asperger Syndrome child is to establish a basis from which I can work together with the school. This may be a useful tool for anyone who is providing a case management role with a child at school.

I plan the time period of my observation so that I can see the child in a number of situations that reflect his school experience. These include teacher-led lessons, independent and group work periods, and recess. When relevant for that child, I observe the lunch period. To accomplish my objective of establishing a shared view of the child, I have found that it is best to do a very thorough observation and report.

The process begins with a description of what could be seen by anyone watching at the same time, although the professional may observe things that another person may not have noted.

1. The description should be such that anyone present would agree that it had occurred.

2. The impressions that follow are then understandable, based on the observations described in the report.

3. The observations and impressions can then lead, also in a very understandable way, to the suggestions and recommendations.

Because of this sequence, the shared information can lead to a better under-standing of the child and acceptance of him. This is my thinking and my goal. When I have other child therapists do the school observation for me, because the child already knows me, I ask that they keep their detailed observations separate from their impressions. Some create a column so impressions can be noted next to the relevant observation, but also remain separate from those observations.

At some point I realized that with these children, who focus so much on details themselves, my own observations and reports are much more detailed. My reports are often more than twice as long as my written reports of school observations of neurotypical children, although the observation time periods were of equal length. I have noticed that this also occurs when another profes-sional has done the observation and report. This is true, despite the fact that the other professional generally has had no prior knowledge of the child or the diagnosis. The details do seem more important in understanding these children. Global descriptions may describe behavior in a way that helps us to understand many children. Global descriptions do not seem to lead to a real understanding of the Asperger child's experience. Yet, while I find that I am only able to make the observations meaningful when I describe them in detail, I try to state my impressions clearly and more succinctly. I then try to follow this with clear recommendations. I want the recommendations to make sense in terms of the child's issues, and to be easy to follow. (See Appendix 2 for specific examples of school observation reports.)

Formal School Meetings

Currently in the United States, formal school meetings are available to address assessment and services for children in the public schools. My primary focus will be on the case management aspect of my role in these meetings as the consultant to the parents or as the child's therapist. I see my role as providing guidance to facilitate understanding of a child's needs and addressing interventions that are helpful to the child. (See Appendix 3 for a brief description of these meetings.)

Preparing for a Meaningful Team Meeting

At the Individual Education Plan (IEP) team meeting the goals for the year are written. Often assessment reports are shared. The specialists from the school present information on the child's current functioning and suggest goals for the next year. If a school observation report is available, the parents and I share this with the team in advance. If there are other reports available from private therapists, these are shared. We request assessment reports from the school prior to the meeting, whenever possible. This enables everyone to give thought to developing meaningful goals and benchmarks. It allows an opportunity for the parents and me to make suggestions for changes based on our understanding of the child.

Brandon

The school district, parents, and I had agreed that Brandon, a third grader who was well ahead of other students in his third grade class in reading and math, had significant difficulty participating in school. He often read material unrelated to the lesson. He had run out of the classroom on several occasions, resulting in concerns for his safety. The following were suggested goals from the language therapist that we had an opportunity to preview prior to the team meeting. We recommended changes we felt would be more meaningful to Brandon.

Original suggested language goals from the school for Brandon

1. *Social pragmatics goal: Increase awareness and use of strategies to assist with problem solving.*

    - Given that a problem has occurred, Brandon will accurately identify the cause of the problem with one prompt 50 per cent of the time.

    - Given that Brandon has identified the cause of the problem, Brandon will generate two possible solutions and the consequences of each solution with minimal adult cueing 80 per cent of the time.

As Brandon's parents and I discussed this goal in preparation for the meeting, we were concerned that Brandon often did not know why his behavior was a problem for others. He did not understand the consequences of his behavior or even that there might be consequences. He did know if someone thought he was bad and was angry with him. We made the following suggestions for the social pragmatics goal.

Revised pragmatics goal

1. *Social pragmatics goal: Increase awareness and use of strategies to assist with problem solving.*

    - When the adult has identified a problematic situation, Brandon will be able to answer the question, "What has happened here?" descriptively from his point of view.

    - Brandon will listen to the adult's view. If it is different from his view, Brandon will understand it as a different perspective. Brandon will be able to choose from possible solutions that are offered to meet his needs and also obey the classroom and safety rules. (For example, Brandon may need a break. He does not want to stay with the class. The teacher thinks that it is not safe or permitted to go outside, because there is no adult supervision. Brandon can go to a safe corner in the classroom or to another location to rest, read, bounce, etc.)

2. *Original abstract language goal: Increase awareness and use of abstract language and thought.*

    - During discussion of a story, Brandon will answer questions such as "What might happen next? What do you think about...?" with one prompt 50 per cent of the time.

    - Brandon will state whether a question has a correct factual answer or asks for his thoughts or opinions with one cue 50 per cent of the time.

Brandon's parents and I discussed this goal before the meeting. We agreed that Brandon did not understand questions that were not factual. To him "What might happen next?" was a factual question and he did not know the answer.

Revised abstract language goal

1. *Brandon will identify questions of fact (who, what, where, when questions) as questions about facts.*

Brandon will identify questions of opinion, possibility, or personal preference as questions that do not have a right or wrong answer.

We felt that knowing the difference between questions that have a right or wrong answer and questions that do not have a right or wrong answer would be a good beginning. If he could do that, he and we might begin to identify his preference for factual questions and difficulty answering opinion, possibility, or personal preference questions.

The team can plan more meaningfully, if we can address the child's needs in a meaningful way. The therapist's understanding of the child can facilitate this. Even academic goals may not reflect the child's needs. Testing may not accurately reflect a child's abilities or disabilities. Some children do not do well in the test situation, but their reading and math abilities are excellent. They may understand correct and incorrect, right and wrong, and good and bad to mean the same thing. They may have difficulty answering if they are not sure or if the tester does not tell them whether they are right. Of course, the tester cannot do that in a formal assessment. Other children score very well on reading comprehension because of their ability to remember factual details, but may have difficulty comprehending all but the most concrete material.

Written language can be an area of difficulty because of handwriting issues or because the child cannot generate ideas for an open-ended topic. One child, who had worked with an educational therapist, had learned to write an acceptable three or four paragraph essay by using a formula that he understood. In the test situation, one of the stimulus pictures happened to fit well with something he understood and he wrote an excellent short essay. Unfortunately, that was rare in real schoolwork and homework situations, in which he could spend hours unable to generate ideas, even with help. Another child did poorly on math timed testing, although he seemed to know the math facts when asked orally. While writing was more difficult, that was not the only problem. He felt overwhelmed when he saw the number of problems on the page. Understanding the meaning of what the child appears to know or appears to have difficulty doing helps establish goals and benchmarks based on that child's needs.

Traditionally, social–emotional and behavioral issues are the areas in which individual child therapists participate at these meetings. It is in these areas that our understanding of the meaning of the child's communication, thinking, and particular needs may be most important. They need to get along with others who are different from them, but their social, emotional, and behavioral functioning may not be accurately assessed by the same measures that are used for neurotypical children. All children are individuals with individual personalities and needs, but neurotypical children are more like each other than like Asperger children, as Lewis told me when he brought me the picture on the cover of this book.

Social and emotional goals for Asperger children can appropriately reflect the need for these children to learn how to tolerate or respond to others. We can try to give them opportunities to participate in group activities that address their interests. We can address their need to understand what is aggressive or mean-spirited teasing, and what is an invitation to interact. It is very important to understand that their spontaneous behavior may seem odd to others, and that these children need to work hard to be conscious of what something may mean to others. Recess is supposed to be a time to relax and play. For these children, an unstructured social time is often a nightmare. If socializing is important, we need to provide structured, supervised opportunities. If a break is important as an opportunity to relax, we may need to allow alternatives to playground recess. These decisions can be best made from the perspective of understanding what we are asking of the child.

One child who used to see me regularly, but now only had occasional appointments, came for an appointment during his lunch hour. He did not like to miss school, but was happy to miss lunch recess. He understood recess as a time he was supposed to play with others. It was noisy. There was too much running around. He just walked around trying to keep away from people until he could return to the structured classroom. I asked him if he knew that recess was the time to take a rest from the class. It certainly did not seem restful for him. We agreed that if he was supposed to rest, he needed something else to do away from all that noise and action. Right now recess sounded more like work than class time for him. Later his mother told me she offered to wait a while before returning him to school. He told her to just bring him back to school right away. When she reminded him it was still lunch recess time, he said that he knew that. He now knew that recess was supposed to be a break time, and he had decided what to do.

"What are you going to do?" his mother asked him.

"I'm going to lie down on one of the benches," he said.

"Someone might ask why you are doing that," his mother said. "What will you say?"

"I'll just tell them I'm resting," he answered.

This child no longer had an IEP, but he did have a 504 plan (see Appendix 3) with some accommodations. Supporting alternative choices for activities was one of the accommodations. When he had choices he sometimes chose to be with others, even though this was work for him. It was no longer an issue of his thinking that he was supposed to be like most people. He was interested in having friends who shared his interests and accepted him. He did not feel comfortable on the playground and was very relieved to have this be acceptable.

Sometimes schools develop specific behavior plans for children. They may even have a behavior specialist develop a plan to address behaviors they wish to change. Many of these children do well with clear expectations, and respond well to prearranged cues. If the language of behavior modification is the language that the team speaks, it can be used to determine interventions that are meaningful in terms of the child's needs as well as the needs of the school environment. If these plans include rewards and deterrents, they need to be effective. If they are not effective, it is not because the child is stubborn or unmotivated. If the plan does not motivate the child, the plan is not adequate and needs to be changed. The parents and therapist can participate in addressing these aspects of a behavioral plan.

The team members, including the parents and outside therapists, can have an opportunity to preview assessment results, recommended goals, and intervention plans prior to the meeting. The actual team meeting can then address goals and interventions in a more meaningful way. The parents can often request reports and recommendations in advance.

Preparing with a Child

With all but very young children, I often prepare for school team meetings or conferences with the child. This may entail as little as making the child aware of the meeting and its purpose in planning to make school a more comfortable place for him to be. It can include exploring in detail the issues that concern the child. Often children prefer to not attend the meeting. It can be difficult trying to listen to and understand all that is covered. When the school insists on the child's presence, it may be acceptable for the child to attend a part of the meeting. The team can make an effort to focus on helping the child understand decisions that are meaningful to him and that will affect him.

When I work with a child individually over a period of time, that child and I prepare for my role in representing his concerns at the meeting. This enables us to clarify the child's perspective and articulate his concerns. It allows us to examine what has improved or is successful, what is difficult, and specific problematic issues. It enriches our work in understanding the child as well as our awareness of another perspective and, perhaps, how to deal with it.

Andrew

Andrew was a sixth grade child whom I had been seeing for over two years. I had attended several school meetings and he was accustomed to helping me to prepare for these. We made a list and reviewed it for part of several sessions prior to the meeting. We organized the list into positives and issues that concerned him. We added information that he felt the team should know. I took notes while we talked. We came up with the following list.

ANDREW'S PREPARATION WITH PAULA FOR THE IEP MEETING

POSITIVES AND IMPROVEMENTS

1. Does more work in class, cooperates more with what the teacher wants done, concentrates more during lecture and demonstration.

2. Still doesn't like how kids act, but this does not bother him as much.

3. Likes older retired playground volunteer and sometimes plays on supervised team during recess. Contact more okay in this situation (pushing with pressure is more comfortable than touching).

4. Has one friend who lives near him and also goes to the resource specialist's class (can't make more friends because you can't say "Hi" to be friendly, you have to say "Hey, Dude" and Andrew does not want to do that).

ISSUES, CONCERNS, AND THINGS THAT ARE HARD

1. *Homework*:

    - Forgets or loses homework.

    - Mom may tell him to do the assignment the wrong way (not the way the teacher wants).

    - The teacher said homework could be reduced to half plus one. For an odd number, that would be the larger half plus one. If there are five questions, the larger "half" is three plus one is four. Four out of five is too much.

2. *Math word problems*: assignment is to solve, explain reasoning, and explain a three-step solution for entire assignment. Andrew can find answer and explain how he gets it. He cannot find three steps and does not see that there are three steps for all the problems. That's not how he gets the answers.

3. *Group project*: everyone loses five points if someone forgets or loses his work. Everyone is mad at him if he forgets. Points can be made up by answering comprehension questions. He sometimes does not have the comprehension answers the teacher wants. They (the others in his group) should not be punished. He is willing to take his punishment if he forgets to do or loses something.

4. The teacher announced that if there is cheating on tests, the students who copy from someone, as well as those whose work is copied, get a zero. It is hard for Andrew to concentrate on his paper if he has to keep looking up to see if anyone is looking at his paper. (I asked if the teacher might mean that you should not show your paper to someone purposely. He was sure she meant more than this. "This teacher means exactly what she says," he explained to me.)

I presented Andrew's list to the team. This enabled us to address issues that were of concern to him, and it provided wonderful examples of his perception of his world. It demonstrated how disturbed he is by the results of his disorganization. Andrew's IEP included organizational goals. His IEP was changed to include organizational support. An adult would check his backpack before he left school, to be sure that he had all his assignments and everything he needed to complete them. His teacher and mother agreed that if he did an assignment as his mother understood it, he would get full credit. If there were five, seven or nine problems or questions on a homework assignment, he could do the larger half and not add one.

It was hoped that the organizational supports would help Andrew keep up on his group assignments. The teacher felt that the children were all well aware that there were opportunities to make up points in group assignments. The teacher said I could explain to Andrew that as long as he was busy working on his test, she did not expect him to watch out for others trying to look at his paper. Andrew's issues with comprehension questions, and with breaking down the math problem solutions the way others do, were not really addressed. At that point, however, it seemed that making people aware that he often has his own way of understanding was all we could do. Andrew was reasonably satisfied with the changes and clarifications. He felt comfortable that his concerns had been addressed well enough.

Informal Collaboration with Teachers and Other School Personnel

While attending formal team meetings can be an important role for the child's therapist, most contact is more informal and occurs on an as-needed basis. If the school knows that the therapist is available by phone, a teacher, a principal, a language therapist, or someone else at the school may be more likely to raise or respond to issues as they occur. These often can be addressed in a short telephone contact. This also supports a collaborative, problem solving approach for everyone involved. On occasion, I have called a teacher during a session with a child. If I am able to reach the teacher, I immediately share that the child is with me, and address his issue.

Andrew, whose IEP preparation was discussed in the previous section, was very disturbed about a long-term assignment he was having difficulty completing. This was an assignment that required a lot of direction and support for him, because it required an understanding of the organization of the material that was very difficult for him. He knew he was not far enough along to complete his report on time. Andrew was convinced that his report would not be accepted by the teacher, because when she originally announced the due date, she said there would be no time extensions. I knew that this kind of time extension was explicitly described in his IEP, and that his teacher had agreed to and supported this.

I first clarified Andrew's perception of this situation and of the teacher's requirements for him. I then attempted to examine the teacher's general directions to the class. Could she have not meant to include him, when she announced that she would not give time extensions? Would she have said, "except if you have an IEP" if she did not mean him? Could she assume he knew that? He was so sure that she did not intend to give him additional time that he did not want to ask, because he knew she had been perfectly clear already. He agreed that I could call her, because he was very sure I wanted to help, but just did not understand.

When I called Andrew's teacher, I explained the situation as Andrew listened. I told her that I needed her help. I knew that Andrew was very clear about her due date directions. She clarified that Andrew would have extra time and heard me tell him that. I wondered if she had been giving general directions to the class, and would want him to know that he has the usual modifications. She would not be making special announcements about modifications. He could check with her when she gives general directions that are different from the agreement she has with him and his parents. Even when she says "no exceptions" she may not mean him. It is very hard for Andrew to understand why someone says "no exceptions" when there are exceptions. It is this inaccurate and unclear way that neurotypicals talk that he may never really understand, except individual circumstance by individual circumstance. However, a brief clarification supports the process of solving these issues as they occur.

An "in the moment" contact like this one can occur when I have a collaborative relationship with a teacher. In other circumstances, a teacher can be contacted when the child is not present. Sometimes a parent can be brought in and I clarify the child's perception and my confusion about the school's intention. The parent can then facilitate clarifying the issue with the child and the teacher or other school personnel. When teachers raise issues and concerns, parents may offer to have them contact a child's therapist, if that option is available.

10

Preparation of Special Materials

Some of the parents in my practice have worked with me to create materials to be used to help their children at school. My role is as a consultant, and we work together to make these materials understandable and useful. One child had a behavior plan that rewarded self-control with stars. His mother recognized it as a "report card" that had its own set of pressures, without necessarily supporting development. We reworded it to acknowledge his awareness of his needs and behaviors, emphasizing what he did (removed himself and listened from his desk away from the group, chewed on acceptable materials, noticed what the teacher was doing before he talked) rather than that he controlled himself and did not do unacceptable things. The shift to what he was to do, rather than what he was not to do, provided a positive focus for the teacher and the child.

Another parent was very concerned about her child's transition to middle school. Aaron learned easily and worked on grade level or above. He had previously been in a special education class because he was unable to remain calm and focused in the mainstream environment. He had tantrums or withdrew completely when overwhelmed. Prior to entering middle school he was maintained in the mainstream with an aide. *Samantha: A Story About Positive Behavioral Support* (Experimental Education Unit 1995) is an excellent video on the development of interventions for a very high functioning autistic child's full inclusion in the mainstream, utilizing a paraprofessional instructional assistant. It was used as a guide to develop interventions and support for this child. Aaron's adjustment, while acceptable in the elementary school setting, was still problematic. The additional stressors of the many more teachers and students in the larger, departmentalized middle school were of concern to the parents, the child, and the school district. His parents and I developed a behavior plan to assist him. They presented this to all the relevant personnel in advance, for consideration at the IEP meeting.

Development of a Behavior Intervention Plan

Many Asperger children are very high functioning and manage in school without assistance, or with informal support or consultation. Some, however, are unable to function in the mainstream, or even in a special education setting, without significant intervention. It is the latter that are more likely to have behavior intervention plans. (Appendix 4 includes a compilation of items from several specific plans that a number of parents and I have prepared and used with their schools.)

Development of a Reference Binder

Another parent in my practice has a young child whose needs required more than could be provided in his mainstream class. He is in a school district that has a number of special needs children fully included in mainstream classrooms, with or without an aide. His mother participated in a task force to address the needs of these children. As part of this project, she developed a reference binder that we worked on together. The purpose was to generate a model that could be prepared individually for these children. (See Appendix 5 for a prototype of this kind of reference binder.) The reference binder is one other support for a collaborative team approach.

Conclusion

With very high functioning Asperger children, case management does not necessarily involve much of what I described in this chapter. For many children we do not use specific materials or even formal intervention plans. These children can still benefit from the availability of even occasional, less formal, collaboration between the school, the parents, and the child's therapist. The underlying purpose is always to facilitate understanding, communication, and an opportunity to support the child's strengths while we meet his needs.

Afterword

Several children that I see in my clinical practice have been very enthusiastic about my writing this book. They want others to learn more about Asperger's. They have suggested that I include specific things that they have told me, things that I have learned about them, and I have done that. Some of the writings of one child, Zach, are particularly germane in illustrating this point.

Zach

Zach, a sixth grade student, has learned to write his English assignments in a way that works well for his Asperger mind and also works very well for the neurotypicals who read what he writes. He has written to explain himself, in much the same way that Lewis drew the picture on the cover of this book.

Zach is a twelve-year-old boy with Asperger Syndrome. He and I have worked together for four years. Writing, knowing what to write as well as the act of writing it down, were very difficult for him. Language therapy was helpful. He learned to develop and express his thoughts well enough to write a paragraph on a specific subject. He had accommodations at school that allowed him to dictate to his mother. He could write a first draft and then read it to his mother, who then wrote it clearly and edited for spelling, grammar, and punctuation.

Once, during the sixth grade, his mother was away. During that time he wrote an essay without her help. It was one and a half pages long, but it was one paragraph. It was apparent that he had done this without help. His teacher's comments were all about the content, which was excellent. She circled a few misspellings, but did not make a comment about the lack of paragraphs. Zach told me that he has not been able to learn when to start a new paragraph. His teacher undoubtedly knew this and did not want to comment on something that she knew he did not understand. He did not need to be made aware of this; he was already aware of it and knew to ask for help. "If I become a writer," he told me, "I'll have to have an editor. That's what editors are for, isn't it?"

This same English teacher gave assignments in which the topic, the form, and specifics to be included were very clearly stated. Sometimes the assignment was to write a poem. Zach liked to write poetry. He understood metaphors and similes, and liked to use them when they were assigned. He understood how to translate a description utilizing a metaphor.

One assignment was to write a poem describing an experience, utilizing various poetic techniques that they had studied. The students were to follow the form of a poem they had read. Zach does not know anyone like him at school, and the behavior of his peers has been upsetting and very difficult for him to understand, especially during the unstructured lunch recess. He wrote a poem to describe that experience.

Wingless

There is a school that I go to where children have wings
and spread them when the lunch bell rings.
Flying high
with greatness in their eyes.
Brrring...brrring...
the next bell rings
Time for the children to fold their wings
and walk into the classroom
as though it was a mummy's tomb.
It's too bad I don't have wings.
Children may see me on the ground
but won't give me a lift
no one that I have found.
Instead they laugh
and cut my heart in half.
Then they fly high
until you can barely see them in the sky.

When I read that poem, I was so moved that I felt like crying. I looked up to see Zach looking intently at me.

"Why does your face look like that when you're reading it?" he asked me.

"Because I am so moved by your poem," I answered.

Zach shook his head pensively. "My Mom looked like that when she read it," he said. "My teacher sometimes looks like that when she talks about my writing."

Our reactions were an enigma to him. He liked that his writing seemed really special to us, but he did not understand our reaction. He certainly knew that he often felt awful during recess or when children said mean things. He was describing that situation in the poem, translating it, using metaphors and similes. The words, however, were not what made him feel the emotion. He could understand if we were impressed by his use of a metaphor or simile. He did not understand why we were feeling what we imagined was his experience.

While Zach would like to be more comfortable with his peers at school, he likes many things about himself. He is comfortable with peers at a summer camp he attends. Most of them are more accepting of him, or at least do not make fun of him. In response to an English assignment to write a rhyming poem about himself, he wrote the following poem.

> I'm nature loving, deep thinking,
> opinionated, and caring
> The son of a nurse and a surgeon
> who's seafaring.
> I live in Los Gatos, an energized,
> growing community
> With my brother, sister, and three pets
> mostly in unity.
> I study different religions and all
> nature (including humans).
> My talent is understanding animals,
> especially my pet Newman.
> I believe in nonviolence and compassion
> for peace and nothing less.
> I'm appreciated for my honesty
> and kindness.

I smiled when I read this poem. I smiled because Zach was describing himself so accurately and positively. I smiled because he said some warm and funny things. Zach wanted to know why I was smiling. He thought, perhaps, that I noticed that he had called his pet Newman, and I knew that he did not have a pet named Newman. He told me that he had needed a little help with ideas for rhyming words, and could not think of something that was accurate. He knows about poetic license, and that it is supposed to be okay to change a word, if it makes the poem work better. He knows, at least, that others think it is okay. It still seems somewhat strange to him, but in this case he was willing to do it. The assignment was due, and he had not come up with another possibility.

It is not easy to know someone whose mind is different from our own. It is easier to know who he is not, than to know who he is. But it is very worth the effort to try. When we do try to understand each other, we both learn a lot.

Professional Services for Children
with Asperger Syndrome

As a child psychotherapist working with Asperger Syndrome children, I have had many opportunities to collaborate with other professionals. This is only a brief overview, from the perspective of my experience, of interventions that may be helpful to these children.

Occupational Therapy

Even before I recognized that I was working with Asperger children, I knew children who used and benefited from occupational therapy (OT). In collaborating with these therapists, I learned that child occupational therapy is based on a developmental approach. A child occupational therapist should have an understanding of sensory and motor development as well as deficits in sensory processing and motor planning. An occupational therapy assessment identifies a child's abilities and difficulties, with an understanding of their importance in development of later skills.

When I began collaborating with occupational therapists, I realized that their interventions are often at the lowest level of need. This amounts to filling in gaps in the base, so the structure that is built on this base can be more solid. I have always appreciated this developmental approach, and find it to be very consistent with the work I do and the way I think about children. Child occupational therapists are taught to find ways to make their interventions positive experiences for the child. I have seen many children who have been in occupational therapy. Almost all of them love their OT appointments. It is my impression that there are at least two reasons for this. First, it is the responsibility of the adult to make the experience positive. Second, the developmentally appropriate level of the intervention results in a successful mastery experience for the child, no matter how significant his difficulties or deficits are.

Years ago, well before I realized all the ways in which occupational therapists could be helpful, I referred children with obvious motor and coordination problems. These could be gross motor or fine motor issues. Sometimes a child did not cross the mid-line, bumped into things, did not seem to know where he was in space, or had significant handwriting difficulties.

Two children I was seeing in psychotherapy for emotional issues had difficulty writing. Both had been in tutoring programs that addressed hand-writing skills and handwriting practice directly, without much success. The children were very frustrated and did not want to go. In both situations, an occu-pational therapy assessment identified upper body weakness. One child's hand-writing improved significantly after she and the therapist worked on upper body strength. In retrospect it seems obvious that someone who has difficulty holding up her upper body would have difficulty with handwriting.

In addition to upper body weakness, the other child also had motor planning issues, which had to be addressed. After that, direct work on handwriting was needed, but this time it was more helpful. He still did not like handwriting, and preferred to use a keyboard. However, his writing abilities improved enough for writing to be a tool when he needed it, rather than a major effort in and of itself.

Later I learned about the role of occupational therapy in sensory processing and managing sensory stimuli. Often Asperger children have difficulty with internal and external sensory mediation. They also frequently need and benefit from appropriate sensory stimulation. As they learn about their needs and how to meet them, the children can help themselves to manage. As their parents understand these needs, they can provide the appropriate equipment, time, and place for the child to meet these needs. Some of the children seem to need to bounce, some to swing. Some need to chew. These behaviors are not necessarily an indication of anxiety, although the behaviors often make others anxious. The opposite may be true. Not having an opportunity to meet these sensory needs may be what makes the child anxious or depressed. Not meeting these needs can lead to behaviors that are even more disturbing to others. This is particularly problematic, because it can lead to the appearance that the child has a serious behavior problem and is "choosing" noncompliance.

Occupational therapists can develop recommendations for parents and schools in addition to their direct work with the child. They can suggest a sensory diet, depending on a specific child's needs. These recommendations support success at school and home. I may recognize that a child is not distracted. He may concentrate better when he is chewing his shirt. The occupational therapist can consult in a way that explains the child's needs and offers specific suggestions or alternatives to meet his oral motor needs. If a child has an Individual Education Plan (IEP) or a 504 Plan (accommodations that can be provided for a child who is not eligible for an IEP), the school or private occupational therapist's suggestions can be an important contribution.

Language Therapy

Collaborating with language therapists who understand Asperger Syndrome is often very supportive to both of our work with the child. In addition the language therapist often has suggestions that aid in planning interventions and support at school.

Those with Asperger Syndrome have so much expressive language that language therapy may not come to mind as an area of need. Yet they do have difficulty with communication, and not only in social and interpersonal situations, although social situations may be the most obviously problematic for the child.

Expressive language and communication are clearly not the same thing. For most of us, our expressive language is a minimal indication of what we understand. Most of us understand (receptive language) considerably more than we can state (expressive language). It came as a surprise to me, when I first worked with Asperger children, to realize that some children can express much more than they understand. All children sometimes say things without understanding the full meanings, to adults or older children, of the specific word or words they have used. However, they still do understand much more than they can articulate.

Asperger Syndrome children can seem to take in language whole, then use it without always understanding it and without knowing the meaning it has to the person with whom they are speaking. Memorizing and then using language, for them, does not require the same level of comprehension it seems to require for typical children. Perhaps this is an example of remembering the parts (words, sentences, or whole stories) without understanding the central concepts. In addition, it seems that their theory of mind issues contribute to their limited ability to know how their statements are received. If you do not understand your own references and those of another person, you cannot have good communication. These are pragmatic language issues.

I began reading about pragmatic language many years ago, to try to understand these issues in my work with children. I discussed what I had learned about pragmatic language with parents, as I described my observations of their child's communication. One of these parents shared this with a friend who was a language therapist with an interest in pragmatic language. This led to a private pragmatic language evaluation and therapy for the child. It was through this experience that I learned that language therapists, who have an understanding for pragmatics and how to process pragmatic language in the moment, can help these children with social and interpersonal communication, as well as language-based learning challenges.

Because clarifying communication is so much a part of my work with the child, the language therapist and I may, at times, be addressing some of the same issues. However, my work is primarily through the relationship. It is not structured except by what happens between the child and me, and by external circumstances I am aware of and that the child and I may address. Through our relationship, as part of our communication, we have many opportunities to address the existence of minds and their differences.

The language therapy is often planned with exercises and tasks that address specific issues and problematic situations. It may address academic issues and social issues, as well as life skills that involve communication. The ability of a language therapist to understand perspective and to process perspective in the moment seems to be one of the keys to the success of the language work. It is also the key to developing a positive relationship with the child. This requires that the therapist be interested in learning the child's perspective and then exploring other perspectives as part of the work. This is necessary, just as it is necessary in my work with these children and in their relationships with their parents and others in their lives. The language therapist is asking the child to work hard in an area that is difficult. The child may not expect success, because he may not expect to understand how others think.

Although language therapists are exposed to the concept of pragmatic language in their training, only those who grasp the meaning of the concept are helpful to these children. If the language therapist talks about teaching pragmatics by practicing or rehearsing situations that may arise in daily life, the therapist may not be dealing with the pragmatic component of the live situation. When the children only practice contrived situations, they can walk out of the therapy room and not recognize the situation they have just practiced, although it is happening right before their eyes. Learning rules for certain situations is an attempt to circumvent not getting the meaning in the moment.

The best outcome with these children will never be a natural feel for the nonverbal or implied meanings in communication. The best result is a recognition of what is understood and what needs to be clarified. It requires consciously paying attention to what others are attending to, and then trying to figure out what is happening.

Along with pragmatics, language therapists also can address comprehension and organizational issues in learning. This includes helping the child to learn strategies or formulas that can aid in creative writing assignments as well as comprehension of literature. The comprehension of literature and essays may not include the layers of meaning that others find. These children need sufficient comprehension to deal with the required reading and sufficient strategies to create an acceptable essay. Because this approach does circumvent some of what is implied in literature, it helps the student to master the work sufficiently. These children also can learn to rely on strategies that can provide some help in

organizing their work according to the teacher's requirements, even if this organization seems arbitrary to them. When modification of assignments is needed,
the language therapist may have specific suggestions.

Group Therapy

In the area in which I practice, we are fortunate to have several options for group
experiences for Asperger children. These children may enjoy and benefit from the
group, if they like the activities, and if they are not expected to be much more
socially competent than they can be. It has been my experience that these
children often want time away from others. It can be stressful to be with others
who reject or criticize them, or who expect them to play in ways that they do not
enjoy. I find that these children often like to be with those who are tolerant of
them and interested in them. That is why adults can be preferred company. Adults
may be interested in or impressed by the way they speak. They know a lot and
often have an adult vocabulary. They do not want to have to try to be someone
other than they are. They seem to know that they are not like others, but they like
to be with people who accept them as they are. They can willingly participate in a
small group, if they feel accepted by the adult and their peers.

Some groups are time limited and address social skills with friends. They are
generally run by psychotherapists for children who have difficulty with social
situations. The groups generally have planned activities and are focused on
learning to be in a peer group. These are particularly successful if the children are
well matched.

Occupational therapists and language therapists also run groups for children,
privately and in schools. For some children a combination of an occupational
therapy activity and pragmatic language can be addressed in a small group. This
requires that the therapist have some knowledge of the occupational therapy
needs and activities as well as an ability to process the language. In our area there
are some opportunities for private small groups throughout the school year, and
part-day summer camps. Some of these are specific activity or interest camps run
by therapists. Children can then choose a session based on their interest in the
activity. In some schools a speech and language therapist or counselor may see
children in social skills groups.

While we adults are often concerned that the Asperger child be able to be
successful in situations with typical peers, which can be very stressful for them,
finding ways to understand what will be seen as appropriate or inappropriate
with typical peers, and surviving these situations, can be enough for these
children. They tend to like to be with children who accept them as they are and
share their interests. This is not surprising. It is true for many people. It is harder,

of course, for these children to find friends who are like them or who like to be with them.

Asperger children do better when they understand what is comfortable for them. They may want to have a friend or friends, and they may want to spend time with their friends. Being together may mean doing separate things for part of the visit. They do need to understand that in most circumstances having a guest or being a guest means being together for the visit. They can also understand that they have a different need, and that is fine if it is acceptable to both children. Their friends can be other children who are like them, or neurotypical children who genuinely like them, children who may share an interest or who are tolerant or even supportive and facilitating with them. Adult-led small groups can be a good start.

On occasion, a child in my practice may have difficulty in a social skills group. Collaboration can be helpful, so that the group therapist and I can respond to the child's issue in a way that is supportive. These children are used to hearing behavior labeled as appropriate or inappropriate. I always find that the experience is most acceptable and meaningful for the child if perspective is the focus. The child's experience is clarified and understood, and the existence of another perspective is then explored, rather than appropriateness.

Specific Educational and Behavioral Interventions

Schools often speak about specific educational and behavioral goals and interventions. This can include a behavior plan. Behavior plans are addressed further in the section on school-related aspects of case management.

Parents often find private educational programs. Some of them evaluate for specific disabilities or weaknesses, and then match the child to a learning program or programs that have been shown to address the skills in question. These programs may or may not be helpful to these children.

Behavior therapy has been found to be very helpful for autistic children, to decrease inappropriate behavior and shape more acceptable behavior. For many children, especially children who would otherwise be much less manageable and more dependent, these interventions can be very helpful. I have seen children gain skills and elicit more positive responses and care from others as a result of intensive behavior therapy interventions.

For the Asperger child, I like to see behavioral interventions that are meaningful to the child, develop the child's ability to observe himself, and enable the child to be a participant in problem solving. I am concerned when a plan is only focused on eliminating or learning a specific behavior, particularly if the child has the capacity to learn to observe himself and others and be a participant in problem solving. Management of behavior may be necessary for the comfort or safety of the child or for others. If it can be addressed successfully by a behavioral intervention, that can be helpful to the child and others in his life. If that can be part of a larger plan that develops coping skills, it is even more useful. The key factor for me is the meaning of the intervention to the child.

It has been my experience that behavior therapists often do not see the kind of therapy that I do as particularly useful. Perhaps we primarily work with a different population. I am happy to participate in the development of a behavior plan to help a child at home or at school. My participation is from my under-standing of the meaning of behavior modification. A behavior modification plan is one that effectively changes behavior in the desired way. By this definition, the child should not be able to fail the plan. If the change is not taking place, the plan has failed the child and the plan needs to be changed. We need to understand the child better to develop an intervention that is more meaningful to this particular child, in order to be more effective. We need to understand whether what we are asking is something the child can do successfully, and then we may need to revisit our goal if it is not.

Psychopharmacology

There is considerable information available about the use of medications with Asperger Syndrome in other books and articles. The Asperger Syndrome children I see often benefit from medication. These children may be seen as having attentional issues, and some may be distractible or hyperactive in addition to their Asperger's. However, often their attentional issues are not those associated with distractibility, as in children with Attention Deficit Disorder. Asperger children can be especially difficult to distract. Distractibility is only one reason for lack of attention. There are other reasons to not pay attention as much as a teacher or someone else requests. They may not be interested in the topic. They may not need review and may be bored by it. They may be paying attention to or thinking about something else.

Asperger children may exhibit symptoms of anxiety and depression. This is often secondary to the stress that life presents as they try to function surrounded by neurotypicals whom they do not understand very well and who do not understand them very well. Anxiety and depression can occur because they often feel overwhelmed. They may be overwhelmed by sensory stimuli. They may be overwhelmed by learning and interpersonal pressures. They may get easily stuck, and perseverate verbally or behaviorally, making problem solving impossible at that time, and leading to a sense of hopelessness.

At this time, the child psychiatrists that I consult with most often prescribe selective serotonin re-uptake inhibitors (SSRIs) for these children, either alone or in combination with another medication. It has been my observation that these medications can lessen the irritation of sensory stimuli and therefore lessen the experience of sensory overload. They can reduce the tendency to perseverate or make it easier for another person to interfere with the perseveration and redirect the child. They can lessen the need for self-soothing behaviors that may comfort these children, but cause others distress. I observe, and children sometimes describe, that with medication they are less frustrated in situations that might otherwise be overwhelming.

Medication may be prescribed by a psychiatrist, a neurologist, or a pediatrician who has had training and experience with the appropriate medications and is comfortable with them. Collaboration with the psychiatrist, or other prescribing physician, can be an important component in monitoring the effects of medication. I communicate with the prescribing physician on an as-needed basis about issues and questions that relate to medications. This is common in child psychotherapy when psychiatric medication as well as psychotherapy is part of the child's treatment. This is particularly important, because I see the child and parents more often than the prescribing physician. In addition, I often have a case management role and may have had contact with school personnel or another therapist.

In collaborating with the physician, I have learned that it is important to be clear as I articulate my own, the parents' and the child's observations of the child and the particular symptoms which the medication is to address. We (the physician, the parents, the child, and I) can then see if the medication is helping in a way that all of us can understand and articulate. The subjective experience of the child on medication is often that he or she has more time to understand and respond consciously to something, rather than react or "melt down" quickly. One child may find that she has time to make choices, to take time out for a break, for example. Another may find that he is less likely to get very angry and want to quit when something is difficult at first.

It is important that the child, with parental encouragement and assistance, be compliant and take the medication as directed. Children are aware that I communicate with their parents and the physician about their medications. This provides another opportunity to address something that is important to the child. Some children are comfortable taking medications. Some are resistant at first, but agree to comply. They may then find that they are relieved when they see that the medication helps them. This is especially true when they perceive, often with adult support, the specific differences that the medication seems to make.

School Observations

The following is an entire School Observation Report of a kindergarten age child. It was completed at the request of his parents, to assist in planning his mainstream school placement. An effort was made to provide descriptions that could be easily visualized and understood by the reader, descriptions and observations that would lead to an understanding of this child's strengths and his needs, as well as a willingness to accept and support him.

School Observation Report

Name: Joey Smith
Parents: Beth and Craig Smith
DOB: 2/28/93
CA: 6 years 1 month
Observation date: March 23, 1999

Identifying information and referral issue

Joey Smith is the six-year-old son of Beth and Craig Smith. He lives with his parents and his nine-year-old sister. Joey attends the pre-kindergarten class at a local school. His parents decided to have him attend this small, structured class after he had been diagnosed with Asperger Syndrome. This was described as his first positive school experience. He had been overwhelmed in preschool and generally unable to participate in any activities. Joey had an Individual Education Plan (IEP) and his parents and school district had agreed to have him enter a mainstream kindergarten the following September. He has been receiving language and occupational therapy services. His parents requested a school observation to assist in educational planning. I was introduced as a visitor to the class, and Joey did not know that I was there to observe him.

Behavioral observations

Joey was observed in Mrs L's class for 2 hours and 45 minutes. During this time he participated in structured, teacher-led small-group activities, lunch, outdoor recess, and a teacher-led class lesson. The class is in a large, open room with tables and a carpeted circle area. Instructional materials and some of the children's work were on the walls. There was an outdoor playground adjacent to the classroom. There were 14 children, the teacher, and an aide, Mrs D, present in the classroom. When I arrived, the children were divided into two groups, each working at a rectangular table with one of the adults. Joey was one of three boys and three girls at a table with Mrs L. His five-year-old neighbor, Sarah, whom he has known since infancy, also attends this class. She was at the other table.

The children at Joey's table were drawing an example of something they know how to do in an outlined box on a paper. The teacher asked each of the children to describe what he/she was drawing. Joey wanted to draw a bird flying, then said he would draw himself flying. He looked up and listened, but did not respond to the teacher's question about whether he could fly. He drew himself standing, but said he was flying. At one point, he made a comment about his neighbor, Sarah. The teacher asked Joey if his neighbor was in his picture. Joey pointed to another child's picture and said his neighbor was in that picture.

The teacher then asked the children to draw a picture of something they cannot do, but would like to do, in another box on the paper. Another child expressed interest in Joey's idea of flying and drew himself flying. Joey said he would like to go to heaven and drew himself in heaven. Several children told him he would have to die to go to heaven. Joey looked up at them as they spoke, but did not respond. He then continued drawing, unperturbed.

Next the teacher led this group in an activity related to categories. The children were each given a worksheet with rows of pictures. They were to cross out the picture that does not belong, such as a dog in a row of vegetables. The teacher noticed Joey as he started crossing out pictures randomly. He stopped and listened as she addressed him by name. She then asked questions that would lead him to understand the assignment, pointing to relevant pictures as she led him through an example. He sometimes paused before answering. Once he understood, he did the entire assignment correctly, and was able to give an explanation for his answer, such as "a dog is not a vegetable."

The final task was to draw a circle around a word that has the same meaning as a word read by the teacher. Again, Joey responded to the teacher as she clarified the assignment directly with him. He almost always responded to his name. He rarely appeared to attend when the teacher was talking to another child at the table, and did not know the information she gave the other child when he was asked about it. Joey did not appear to listen to or respond to the statements made by other children. He attended to his own paper, or to the teacher when she addressed him individually. Once again, when he understood the assignment, it seemed that he could do it easily.

Joey and his group were asked to go to the other table. Joey continued sitting. His neighborhood friend, Sarah, came to Mrs L's table. She directed Joey to the other table. Joey responded by going and starting to work there. This was their only interaction. They were generally involved in different activities.

Joey began coloring a playground scene. The children were to color pictures of things that could be found in a park. These small drawings were on a larger paper with pictures of things that would and things that would not be appropriate in a park. Each child was given a paper for his or her park. The children were to cut out and paste their colored pictures in appropriate places on their picture. Then they were to write "Park," capital "P", lowercase "p" and their names on the paper. Mrs D was available to the children if they needed her. She helped them mount the pictures on construction paper when they were finished. Some children talked to each other as they worked. When they were finished they were to go to a free play area and choose an activity. Joey seemed familiar with the task. He concentrated on his paper, and did the assignment correctly. When he finished, he wandered around the room by himself.

During the small-group activities, Joey generally sat still and worked parallel to others. He did not interact with them or watch them. He seemed intent on his work. He seemed comfortable with the pencil-paper, drawing, and cutting tasks. When he talked, he spoke clearly and often in complete sentences. During clean-up time, Joey initially joined some of the children who were cleaning up. Children were milling around in a small space as they cleaned up. Joey backed away. He remained on the periphery of the group.

The children were to line up to wash their hands before lunch. Joey stood in line with several boys. The boy behind him put his arm around Joey and shook him playfully. Joey kept repeating, "Why did you do that to me?" The boy looked confused. The boy then turned to another boy behind him and playfully grabbed his hands. They looked at each other questioningly, and then they both laughed. Those boys continued to hold each other's hands, jumping as they shook each other playfully. Joey moved so there was more space between him and the jumping, laughing boys.

The children ate at tables with benches for seats. Some of the children were talking as they ate. Joey concentrated on eating. After eating, Joey and the other children went to the playground for recess. He ran around the edges and through the play area. Occasionally he ran near another child, but he never made contact. One child was playing by herself near a climbing structure, and Joey sat near her for a while doing a parallel activity. He did not say or do anything that indicated recognition of her presence.

Several of the children were planning a chase game. They discussed who would be "it" and then began playing. They did not include Joey, and he did not show any interest in joining them. Meanwhile, Joey was dragging a small plastic molded slide together with another to form a building. He asked some of the girls to join him to play house. Eventually several girls started playing together nearby. He noticed them and seemed satisfied to play near them. He filled a pot with sand and dumped it out several times. He was sitting on the ground with his back to the girls.

The children lined up to return to the classroom for an instructional period. They sat at tables for a teacher-led lesson about famous places. They were shown a new picture of something they had not seen before, the Washington Monument, and read a paragraph of information about it. Joey was very attentive. Next they reviewed pictures they had seen before. They were asked to either name the place or tell something about it. Joey raised his hand. When he was called on, he was quiet for a while. The teacher waited patiently while Joey thought. He answered correctly with very complete information (so exact, I wondered if his were the very words in the paragraph that had been read when that picture was initially presented). When others were answering, Joey looked preoccupied. He stayed in his chair, but fidgeted with the chair and only appeared to be attending intermittently. When the child next to him touched his head, he responded by pulling back and moving away.

Joey's teacher and her aide both indicated that the day I observed was a typical school day for Joey.

Impressions

Throughout the observation, Joey generally appeared comfortable with the class. He seems to benefit from a structured, predictable classroom environment, including specific assignments with attentive reminders and clarification, and redirection as needed. He also benefits from individual attention, instruction, and patience from his teacher. He sometimes needed time to access information he already knew. The use of a directive, calm teaching approach seems to be particularly important for him.

As noted, there were intermittent times when Joey appeared disconnected and preoccupied. He appeared to have the most difficulty when he did not have a specific assignment that he understood and when confronted with less structured situations. Joey also seemed preoccupied during instructional time when the material was reviewed or when he was not addressed individually, by name. As a result, his responses were, at times, inappropriate to the situation. He was compliant with all teacher requests, but sometimes began without understanding the assignment.

Joey seemed overwhelmed by the physical contact or closeness that some of the boys engage in. He misinterpreted social situations that included physically close play, and appeared to be confused by what he may have assumed was negative intent from others. There were very few unstructured situations indoors, and that seemed a good fit for this child.

During recess, Joey was aware of the other children, at times seemed to want them near him, but avoided contact that overwhelmed him. He did not engage in mutually developed interactive play. He did not exhibit the social play skills, during unstructured recess time, that are important to feel safe and behave appropriately in recess situations, such as might be found on a larger playground used by many children at the same time.

Recommendations for kindergarten
CLASSROOM PLACEMENT

Considering the observation findings, it appears that Joey would benefit from a structured mainstream classroom setting, as long as support services and accommodations are available. A non-reactive, supportive, and yet directive teaching approach would be beneficial. In other words, a teacher whose classroom routine is structured and predictable, and who is empathic and not rigid, would be best. The adjustment to the new school may be difficult, and having his neighbor, Sarah, in his class for kindergarten might be supportive to him. He does respond to her, and yet is not particularly dependent on her. This is not likely to place undue pressure or responsibility on her.

SUPPORT SERVICES AND ACCOMMODATIONS

Resource support in the classroom and in the resource room (as a safe haven or to address specific goals), along with language therapy and occupational therapy and/or adaptive PE to address sensory, motor, and pragmatic issues, should be sufficient to support Joey in a mainstream environment. These supports may be even more important in first grade.

CLASSROOM INTERVENTION STRATEGIES

Classroom intervention strategies may be needed for a long time. The teacher, as well as Joey, will experience success if they recognize and accept this support and direction as necessary and helpful.

1. Cue Joey verbally by saying his name, and nonverbally by pointing after getting his attention.

2.   Clarify Joey's understanding of assignments.

3.   Allow him to remove himself or suggest specific tasks (such as during clean-up) that do not require Joey to be in less structured, physically close situations with a lot of movement.

4.   Allow extra time, when Joey needs it, to retrieve his response after raising his hand. (The need for this can be made explicit to Joey and others, in an informational and nonjudgmental manner.)

5.   During review, a combination of redirection and allowing him to drift off or fidget may be most helpful. (He seems very attentive to new material, especially if it is factual. If he knows something already, it may not interest him or benefit him to have to review it multiple times. He should not have to maintain an attentive demeanor during these reviews, as long as he is not disturbing anyone.)

A PRAGMATIC LANGUAGE OR SOCIAL SKILLS GROUP

A small group could provide an opportunity to make Joey more aware of his behavior, its meaning to him, as well as its meaning to others.

1.   Develop an awareness that there may be more than one perspective, such as what an action means to him, what the other child meant. (For example, shaking each other is friendly and fun to the other child. He does not like it. He needs time to think. Others may think his pause before talking means it is their turn to talk.)

2.   An opportunity to know and explain himself. (For example, he can identify that he does not like to be suddenly grabbed. He can say "I don't want to play this way." He needs time to remember something and can sometimes say or at least recognize, "Wait, I need time to remember.")

RECESS AND PE

It is important that physical activities and free play not be so overwhelming that Joey does not feel safe at school, as has happened in the past.

1.   Allow comfortable alternatives to high energy, physically close situations, including alternatives to the playground during recess, if he needs this.

2.   Consider OT recommendations for adaptive or regular PE placement and activities.

The Observation Report about Joey was first presented to the current school to determine whether it was consistent with their experience. It was, and it provided a clearer articulation of the interventions that were working. Teachers often find it easier to continue strategies, and to see them as effective, if they realize that it is acceptable and even desirable to cue the child as needed. This is something we wanted the new mainstream kindergarten to accept. A teacher may feel that she must prepare the child to function more independently or to become more socially adept. If this is more than the child is capable of doing, both will be disappointed and discouraged. The child may become very anxious and unhappy at school.

Joey's Observation Report was primarily prepared to use with the new school in planning for Joey's transition to kindergarten. The school psychologist made a brief visit to observe Joey in his current school to determine current functioning and continued eligibility for accommodations and support. We wanted to add to this by describing detailed observations that could then be recognized if they were consistent with the new teacher's observations of Joey. We wanted to present the strategies that would seem sensible and effective to the teacher, and support her ongoing use of them.

Sean

The following is the summary of another child's school observation. Sean was entering kindergarten. He was taking medication and receiving a number of therapeutic interventions. The medications and interventions addressed his perseverative behavior and talk. They also somewhat diminished his reactions to sensory stimuli. I was asked to consult with his parents, and we would consider individual treatment at a later date. I completed a school observation as the first step to working with the family and school personnel. The following summary addresses aspects of my observations and impressions that were important in gaining agreement on his functioning and on appropriate interventions and support in a mainstream placement.

Sean was a five-and-a-half-year-old-boy who had attended a special day preschool class in his school district. Sean was diagnosed with Asperger Syndrome in a developmental/mental health assessment when he was four years old. His parents consulted with me about his needs in general. They were especially concerned about providing appropriate interventions at school. Sean had been overwhelmed and unresponsive to directions in the classroom. We knew that his behavior had improved. He was more compliant, but we wanted to plan school interventions that address general learning and developmental needs, as well as behavior. Sean did not know me when I observed in his summer school class. An aide was working with him individually in the summer program when I observed.

During that observation, I found that Sean appeared comfortable in the class, although he often seemed unaware of what was going on around him. He relied on very specific and concrete directions with attentive reminders, clarification, and redirection to participate in most activities.

Sean rarely seemed aware of general directions or explanations. However, he did at times have a delayed awareness of an aspect of what was communicated. His occasional comments were often tangential or no longer relevant. At times he had a delayed response to a request. When that occurred, it seemed that he might have needed extra time to process and/or to respond. Sean did not give observable indications that he was attending during that process. The only evidence that he had heard was a delayed response, when that occurred. Often he appeared to be chewing, even when nothing was in his mouth. Once in a while he held his hands over his ears in response to a noise.

Sean attended to his aide whenever she spoke to him, and always looked up if he was aware that she was approaching. He always followed her directions. I noticed that when she asked a question, such as "Did you wash your hands?" he responded with what he thought was the expected "right answer" rather than what was factually correct. I felt that it was unlikely that he recognized the difference between questions that ask for a factually accurate description of what occurred and those that quiz the child regarding his knowledge. In the first case, guessing what the adult wants to hear may be considered lying. In the second case, guessing the expected answer, if you are not sure, is appropriate and encouraged. Most children learn to understand these subtleties as they develop, without a great deal of explanation.

I noticed that there were many times when Sean appeared disconnected from what was happening. He sometimes needed reminders, but often redirected himself to appropriate observable behavior, such as sitting quietly with his hands in his lap. However, he appeared to be unaware of what the class was doing. Sean seemed preoccupied during instructional time when he was not addressed by name. He was unaware of the context and his occasional comments or responses were often irrelevant or inappropriate to the situation. At times during circle he appeared to be reading unrelated material posted on a nearby wall. It was apparent that Sean wanted to please. He was compliant with all teacher requests, but did not seem to understand the larger context of the activity or lesson. When he did understand what he was to do, he focused intently for a while and could refocus himself, often without cueing. It was clear that Sean had learned behaviors that looked appropriate and were not distracting to others, whether or not he understood.

Sean had little apparent awareness of most of the children's interactions. During free play he occasionally avoided contact that overwhelmed him, but generally seemed comfortable with the presence of the other children. He did not know how to engage in interactive or even parallel play. He did not exhibit social play skills during unstructured playtime and managed to be by himself even with many other children playing around him.

I was very concerned that Sean's educational placement and intervention plan should address his cognitive and developmental needs, especially in light of his improved behavior. He already knew how to read and a fair amount of basic math. His behavior did not make his presence a problem for other children or adults. He had a desire to please adults. Sean's parents and I wanted his educational placement and intervention plan to address his cognitive and communication issues in a way that was meaningful to him. This would mean a focus on developing the concepts that underlie and facilitate learning in a classroom. After the observation, we developed a list of suggested goals to bring to a team meeting. Everyone who would attend that meeting had an opportunity to read my observation report and our ideas for goals before the meeting. Because Sean had learned that he was expected to look attentive, without understanding why, we developed the following list.

Suggested goals for Sean

The goals could include, but are not limited to, the following:

1. Recognize his own and others' cues to attend to verbal communication (currently Sean only consistently responds to his aide's voice or his teacher when she addresses him by name).

2. Recognize (with a cue) that a direction or simple sequence of directions is being given, listen to them, and then repeat them back for confirmation before proceeding.

3. Recognize when he is attending and when he is not, and asking when he needs a break from attending.

4. Learning to understand concrete questions and how to respond to them (including whether the questioner is asking a question for information or knows the answer and wants to know if Sean knows it).

5. Recognizing that there is a topic, and what it is.

Goals like these address awareness first. They then address comprehension of the concepts that would enable Sean to learn in a classroom setting. They are not easy to achieve. We wanted to be prepared to address specific interventions that could support these goals. For Sean, to be aware when he is listening to the teacher and when he is not, and to know if she is giving directions or information, would be a good start.

Classroom placement, support services, and accommodations

The following recommendations were made:

1. Sean would benefit from a structured classroom setting with the continued use of an individual instructional assistant. A teacher with a directive, calm teaching style and a very predictable class routine would be best, if the teacher is also flexible (willing to learn about Sean and accommodate his needs).

2. Language and occupational therapy services can be utilized in planning classroom goals, accommodations and strategies that could be implemented by the teacher and instructional assistant. Small group and individual pullout programs should be utilized when appropriate.

3. Sean would benefit from the availability of a place to retreat in the classroom when he needs a break from the stress of attending and trying to comprehend. When it does not come naturally, thinking about what is happening takes intense concentration and is exhausting. A safe haven outside the classroom, such as the resource room, where he can work away from the larger classroom can be considered at some point. The aide can help Sean utilize these and reorient him when they return to the classroom.

We wanted to facilitate the work of the school team and outside resource providers in the development of specific ideas for interventions. We developed a list of suggestions that we also shared with the team in advance.

Specific interventions to support the goals for Sean

The following list of suggestions was drawn up to facilitate the achievement of Sean's goals.

1. In very simple words and a calm, nonjudgmental, informational tone of voice tell Sean what you observe him doing and what others are doing (a "verbal mirror"). Utilize an actual mirror for the adult and Sean to observe and describe (simply) both of their expressions, responses, etc. Another child can be included in this activity.

2. Tell Sean to listen for "directions" (when the teacher is telling the students what to do) and "information" (the teacher is explaining facts

about something). Tell him the topic. Cue him to listen for directions (or other information) from the teacher or another child. Have him identify and repeat directions, so that it is clear that he understands them (including the sequence of steps when relevant). Have him repeat the topic.

3. As Sean learns that his job is to listen for information or directions (not just behave appropriately), he may find the intensity of this exhausting or overwhelming. Those times should be identified, so he can learn to identify them. Provide a place to retreat or an OT activity (such as chewing something appropriate, bouncing, jumping, running, etc.) to help him modulate his responses and meet his needs.

4. Individually and in a small group, practice having Sean recognize concrete (who, what, when) questions. He needs to learn that he can answer, guess, or say he does not know. By demonstration and practice, teach Sean to recognize questions that request that he describe what actually occurred. The "right answer" is the accurate answer (he did not wash his hands), not what the adult wanted him to have done.

5. Tell Sean when there is a simple topic for a lesson or discussion (such as how to make cookies, countries in North America, animals in the ocean, the specific name of an activity or game) and confirm that he knows it. When possible, subsequent comments and cueing can be identified simply by the topic name or how they relate to it (measure and stir to make cookies, Canada is on the map).

In addition, the following may be generally helpful in working with Sean:

1. Obtain Sean's attention by using his name and/or an agreed-upon signal such as touching his shoulder and pointing to the relevant stimulus.

2. Allow extra time for his response if you feel that he understands the question or request.

3. Provide additional cues or information (the briefest, most relevant part of the question or request) when he does not seem to understand or when he does not respond after a short wait.

4. Recognize and verbalize what Sean did right (such as said accurately what happened, said "I don't know" if he does not know, listened and repeated directions).

5. Provide a daily checklist of very specific items for him to review with his aide at relevant times during the day (e.g., knew teacher was giving

directions, listened to directions, repeated directions, followed directions). This is especially useful for both Sean and the adult, to monitor his progress and plan new strategies for those things he does not understand.

From this perspective, it was easy for everyone on the team to recognize that Sean's improved behavior did not reflect understanding of communications in the classroom. Having manageable behavior would not be an adequate solution, since it would not address his needs. Sean's parents and I knew that all of these interventions would probably not be used regularly. Just as Sean needed to begin to be aware of when the teacher was talking and whether he was listening, the adults needed to be aware of when Sean understood and when he did not.

Formal School Meetings

Other publications provide complete descriptions of the Student Study Team, Individual Education Plan (IEP), and other formal public school processes. The following is only intended to be a very brief description.

Student Study Team

A parent or teacher may request a Student Study Team (SST) meeting. This meeting provides an arena for identifying strengths and areas of concern. The result can be informal planning, informal support and minor accommodations, or a recommendation for an assessment to determine eligibility for an IEP and for additional services. Sometimes parents have outside assessment reports that can be shared with the school to assist in planning.

Individual Education Plan

An Individual Education Plan (IEP) is developed by a team made up of an administrator (often the principal), specialists from the school, and the parents. Parents may bring advisors or advocates to these meetings, and often parents ask me to attend. Subsequent IEP team meetings occur annually, unless requested more frequently, and may include the child, but the child is not generally present for the first meeting. Older children may be required to be present, but younger children often prefer to hear the results. The entire process can be overwhelming and hard to understand.

The IEP team must first determine whether a child qualifies for an IEP according to legal guidelines. Children with Asperger Syndrome may qualify if they have a specific learning disability. Sometimes pragmatic language issues can be demonstrated, and the child is determined to qualify based on a language therapist's assessment. Some children have significant deficits in written language. Sometimes a child qualifies based on an autism spectrum diagnosis that significantly affects school functioning.

Once eligibility has been determined, the team determines goals and benchmarks, as well as accommodations. Many of these are specific academic, social–emotional, and behavioral goals and benchmarks. This may, and often does, include organizational goals. I try to focus my contribution in the area of articulating specific cognitive goals that relate to the academic goals. I also try to contribute to stating language and communication goals in a way that addresses the cognitive issues underlying the pragmatic language deficits. I want this to be more than a basis for measuring growth on standardized tests. I find the plan much more meaningful if we articulate very concrete and easy-to-understand interventions that support the implementation of the goals.

504 Plan

In California, children who do not meet eligibility requirements for an IEP may be eligible for appropriate accommodations through what is known as a 504 Plan. If a child who has been diagnosed with Asperger Syndrome is doing relatively well at school, but needs accommodations to support his success at school, a 504 Plan can be put into place. This is only effective, however, if the school is willing to follow through with meaningful support, interventions, and accommodations.

Items for Consideration when Developing a Behavior Plan

For children who need and respond to a behavior plan, a very simple plan that addresses a few behaviors and interventions is adequate. Anything more is too overwhelming to be useful to the people implementing the plan. The following is a compilation of items from a number of behavior plans. Much more is included than would be appropriate for use with one child. Even if many items seem to apply, it is best to select a few meaningful and manageable areas.

Suggestions for Inclusion in a Child's Behavior Plan

Behavior intervention plan for (child's name) grade —

Begin the plan with a list of items included, such as:

- Problematic behaviors
- Intervention strategies that may be used to affect a given behavior (A brief commentary about the child could be inserted at whatever point seems most meaningful.)
- Information and interventions regarding interactions with peers and adults
- Program suggestions
- Criteria for evaluation and review.

PROBLEMATIC BEHAVIORS

Examples of behaviors that a child may need to control, behaviors that need to be fostered, and behaviors that need modifying to a more acceptable form: *an actual plan should only include the most relevant.*

1. Difficulty attending to class (verbal) discussions.

2. Poor or minimal response to verbal instructions given to the group or even to him directly, such as prepare for or put away an activity, number your paper, etc.

3. Does not stay on task once an assignment is given.

4. Difficulty getting back to work on an interrupted task.

5. Does not ask for help. He may not be cognizant of the fact that he needs help and even if he is, he may not know what exactly it is that he does not understand.

6. Not bringing items home from school in response to teacher's verbal direction.

7. Fidgeting (understanding that some amount of this may be a coping or soothing strategy and therefore tolerating it will help the child.)

8. Calling out (note frequency and whether on or off topic.)

9. Commenting off topic (note frequency.)

10. Inappropriate interaction with other children (example.)

11. Isolation at lunch or recess (explanation or example, such as: some of this is child's way of winding down after the demands of the classroom and may need to be accepted; some may be a result of his inability to interact, and may cause symptoms of depression.)

12. Inability to have spontaneous interaction with peers.

13. Mumbling, talking to himself out loud.

INTERVENTION STRATEGIES

Examples of possible strategies are included. All strategies should be agreed upon and implemented at school and, when appropriate, at home.

1. *Visual cues* (cards or other agreed-upon cues)

    Briefly state the purpose, such as to give visual reminders or assistance if child responds better to visual reminders or "cueing" than he does to verbal instructions or reminders. Cues can be used as reminders of something (he needs to do or not do, as the case may be), or to help him to carry out a series of steps. They can later be used independently by him.

Laminated cards could contain a word or other cue indicating the desired behavior, or steps for a procedure or assignment. If several cards are used, they might be color coded, perhaps to indicate categories of behaviors (e.g., academic, listening, staying on task, etc.) Some examples for cards are:

- Body facing speaker
- Keep working
- Line up
- Put homework folder into backpack
- Steps for a specific assignment, e.g. writing a paragraph.

2. *Praise, feedback, and tracking behavior*

Purpose: provide child with positive information *that is meaningful to him* (can be recognition, appreciation) when he exhibits desired behaviors as well as follows cues given to him, and *help him become more aware of his performance* (including how what happened during the day affected him.)

Ways to give child EFFECTIVE positive feedback and encouragement include providing (a) *a clear set of goals and expectations;* (b) *rewarding consistency* (if a reward program is meaningful or appreciated by him.) Feedback needs to be meaningful to child and should be:

- *Specific* – that is, notice and comment on specific behavior. For example, he followed a specific cue and accomplished the behavior or task.
- *Immediate* or as soon as possible, so that he clearly knows what you are referring to.
- In order to be *successful and reinforcing*, everyone working with the child at school and at home, and the child himself, needs to be clear as to what specific behaviors we are trying to effect, and how. The child needs to know exactly what is expected of him.

Insert (This could be inserted here, or at any point that seems meaningful, based on what information or suggestions come before or after.) A commentary regarding the specific child, including:

- The child's current performance and ways in which it varies (such as at different times of the day, and why, if you know).

- Ways the child relates to time, including past and future events (such as whether the child sees any relationship between past, current, and future events).

- Ways the child responds to directions, rewards, etc.

- What the child needs and responds to, or does not respond to, when stressed (such as does or does not respond to redirection, needs time out or time alone).

- When it is useful or not useful to speak to him about what happened and how to acknowledge his position or experience (for example, "I know you can do it!" may contradict his feelings at the time; he may need to hear, "You don't want to do this right now, do you?" or "This is difficult for you right now, isn't it?".)

- Specific needs for assistance that have or could help him to function and learn (such as someone available to keep a daily record of his performance with him, someone and some place available as a safe haven, someone to help organize and pack his homework).

3. *Calming / refocusing*

Purpose: to provide the child with ways to get himself back on track. An effort should be made to determine why he is having trouble following the rules, staying on task, keeping his body in check, controlling his impulses, etc. Depending on the cause, the following strategies can be employed.

(a) Cause: upset because child seems to be overstimulated. Possible ways to help the child:

- OT activity

- opportunity to complete the work in a quieter location

- allow him another means to complete the task such as dictating answers.

(b) Cause: upset because he does not understand, is having difficulty with, or has an inability to break down and coordinate steps of the work at hand. Possible ways to help the child:

- determining whether or not he understands the task, if it is extra difficult for him and may require assistance, if he needs a quiet place to screen out distractions

- use his sequence cards

- decide what he can do (not lowering the bar, but modifying the teaching strategy).

4. *Social stories* (Gray 1994, 2000)

Purpose: to improve or change specific behaviors related to specific situations. Social stories may not be appropriate for behaviors that are of a more general nature. The stories in this book and Carol Gray's *Social Stories Kit* (Gray 1994, Ch. 25) offer assistance for *writing specific stories to address specific issues*. Consult with and include so that they can (a) carry this over to child's home environment; (b) reinforce and talk about it as a family. The behaviors that might be addressed could be:

- talking to other children on the playground

- talking to children in line to go into the class or at lunch (suggestions for things to say or ask)

- joining in a game

- asking the teacher for help.

INTERACTING WITH OTHERS

To be successful in school, and elsewhere, the child must learn some basic rules of interaction with those around him. While acceptable academic work and staying on task are important, without some basic social skills the child will become more and more isolated. In addition, problems in the social realm spill over into classroom behavior, depression, and anxiety. This is also relevant as it pertains to bullying and teasing that are inevitable.

1. *Social skills*

When someone is available to facilitate, these are some of the social skills the child could work on in real-life situations:

- volume control

- body space

- when it is/is not appropriate to interrupt
- how to join in a conversation
- how to determine if the person you're speaking to wants to talk about your subject.

2. *Other opportunities to help the child in the classroom*

- The child's parent(s) could talk to other students about Asperger's in general, and this child in particular, to encourage and support their ability to be compassionate and helpful. Students could ask questions since they are understandably curious. Some children are naturally nurturing and caring and get great satisfaction out of helping someone like this child. This serves to enrich the child who is lending a hand as well as the child who is being helped.

- A "circle of friends" – two or three classmates who are willing to take the child under their wing – could be established. An adult could use such an opportunity to help the child with conversational skills such as learning about his mentors (their favorite computer games, whether or not they have siblings) and encourage or cue the child to ask for clarification or help from his classmates.

3. *Lunch recess*

Some percentage of the child's recess could be used for social skills work depending on how his day is going in the classroom. Recess is a time to unwind, so he should be able to choose to be with others or to have an acceptable alternative available.

GENERAL PROGRAM SUGGESTIONS

Simple changes in everyday school routines and assignments could have significant impact.

1. *Schedule*: This child could benefit from having a written schedule of his school day. He should preview the day's schedule and note any changes that will apply to the current day (e.g., assemblies, special projects, trips to the library, PE).

2. *Seating*: This child will benefit from sitting nearer to "front and center."

3. *Transition times*: This child responds to a warning in advance of transition times. The use of a cue card or watch might be an option.

4. *Timed assignments*: Timed assignments might need to be modified or eliminated.

5. *Alternative work location*: This child may be able to work in a quiet location if he is unable to screen out distractions and noise.

6. *Safe haven*: This child may need to have a place to go if he is particularly agitated and needs to calm down. This is not a punishment, but a place for him to relax and pull himself together.

7. *Academic opportunity*: This child could be with children who are performing at his academic level even if it means a change of classroom. An example would be to have him go to another classroom for reading or math. Another example would be to allow him to learn a new concept by observing or from a computer program, rather than participation in class discussion.

Developing a Reference Binder

With some modifications, the following is a fairly complete sample of a reference binder developed with a parent for an Asperger child in a mainstream classroom. It is now being used to facilitate integration of a special needs child in the mainstream. While some of the descriptions in this generalized sample may seem somewhat complex, the actual reference binder is very accessible and easy to understand. Each item in both sections is on a separate page. Some of the sections are printed on colored paper and the binder can be set up with color tabs for easy use.

Table of contents

Section 1

> General overview of child
> Child's weekly schedule
> Occupational therapy interventions
> Speech/language interventions
> List of contacts
> Current Individual Education Program (IEP)
> Progress forms

Section 2

> General article about the child's issue
> Related websites and books
> Related terms
> Possible interventions and support approaches
> Guidelines and ideas for communication
> District resource list
> Narrative regarding the process for IEP
> Appendix of forms

General Overview of Child

Description

The first page (or two) of this document is to be tailored specifically to the child. It quickly explains the classroom situation for the teacher and aide (if applicable) as well as for a substitute teacher or aide. Recommended areas for inclusion in the summary include the following:

1. Paragraph about what the child's diagnosis (or challenge) is, and how the child's challenge presents itself.

2. Bullet points regarding specific behavior and what to expect in the classroom. May include items from occupational therapy (OT) and speech and language therapy as well as other interventions.

3. Specific interventions for challenging times during the day.

4. Intervention approach to teaching or guiding the child.

5. Specific reporting requirements (such as checklists) and responsible party (aide or student) when applicable.

Purpose

This is a reference for the primary teacher and aide, but also a resource for substitute teachers and aides so that they will be able to step in and use simple intervention approaches with the student. This will not only make things much easier and simpler for the substitute, but should also provide more continuity for the student and make the student more successful when dealing with change.

Responsible party

This document could be written by the parent, intervention specialist, aide, privately provided specialist, previous or current teacher. If one person creates the summary, whenever possible it should be the person who is most informed about the child and the classroom situation. It will be most accurate if a number of the listed parties have input into the document, though for practicality's sake, that may not always be possible.

General Overview (Example)

Re: Joe (A child with Asperger Syndrome)

Joe does not know (or does know) that the aide is for him. Other parents may be (or may not be) aware that there is an aide supporting this child, and most (do or do not) know what the child's issues are. Please (do or do not) refer to the child's condition with others connected to the class, besides his teacher or his parents. (Please do not, or you may) bring up the diagnostic name when others are around.

Overall summary

Joe is a high functioning child with Asperger Syndrome. We try to use prompts to help him understand why something is going on, so that eventually he will be able to follow the cues on his own. We are not focusing on teaching him the rules, but are focused on his understanding what supports the rules. He can easily learn the rules, but that will not help him later when more independent thinking is expected of him in higher grades. We are working on the bigger picture, but need to do it in small steps so that he will learn to bridge the gaps. Joe is:

- Very visually stimulated and will often look down while the teacher is speaking. Generally, he is still listening. It is less overwhelming for him to not look.

- Working on fine motor skills. He loves to write words and may try to rush through the exercise. We prepare some craft project work ahead of time so that he can do a better job and not be rushed during craft project and center times.

- More distracted during transition times and may forget to face the teacher.

- Apt to stop what he is doing and stare for a while. He is thinking and we redirect him if it has been a minute or so. Sometimes he is making sense of and thinking about the activity. He may be relating it to something else of interest to him, although his reference may seem tangential to us. Sometimes he may not understand or be interested in the topic.

- Vocal and often wants to sing or talk while doing work. When this becomes too distracting, ask him to get chewing gum (or another chewing substance or object) from his backpack so that he has something to do with his mouth.

- Good with words, but not able to process directions as quickly as typical children. Using simple words will make it easier for him. He may need a visual example so he can learn it his own way, rather than following the verbal explanation. He rarely says that he does not understand, or asks for an explanation. Intervene if he is staring for a long time. Ask something similar to "What do you need to do next?" or "Have you finished this page?"

Specific interventions
BEFORE CIRCLE TIME OR SIMILAR TEACHER-DIRECTED ACTIVITY

Tell him, or provide a cue card that says, essentially, "This is the time to listen to the teacher. After circle time I will ask you what she said."

AFTER CIRCLE TIME OR SIMILAR ACTIVITY

If Joe does not follow the directions and proceed to the next activity with the other children, ask him what the teacher said. If he does not respond or says "I don't know," ask him "What are the other children doing?" This will direct him to look at what others are doing to prepare for the next activity. It will help him learn that what others are doing is relevant and can be a way to cue himself.

RECESS AND LUNCH/RECESS

List possible interventions or accommodations here, so that it is clear what support is provided and what alternative activities the child may engage in during these periods. If these accommodations are explained, the child and a substitute teacher will be able to avoid many potential misunderstandings. For example, Joe may go to the computer lab or the library after finishing lunch.

Specific intervention approach
PROBLEM SOLVING DURING THE DAY – OUR INTERVENTION APPROACH

(This intervention strategy is more difficult to follow consistently when there are substitutes. However, this intervention is needed to help Joe get to the next level of social understanding. If there is a specific problem in class, the parent or appropriate intervention specialist can write out a sample that fits the problem, to provide a consistent approach from day to day. The parent, intervention specialist, teacher, and aide can meet as needed to develop meaningful samples.)

During a moment when Joe is not following what he should be doing or is not getting the intent of an event or a behavior, Joe needs someone else to clarify:

(a)   what is going on or what his needs are (singing, chewing, his body faced away from a reader)

(b)   what the needs of the others are at that moment

(c)   what might be appropriate solutions.

The aide should discuss this with him when the actual event is occurring. The clarification and discussion must take place at the time of the event for the conversation to help him learn what is appropriate and what to do (for example, if Joe is facing 90 degrees away from the teacher while she is reading a book). There are several levels of understanding, and we will break out each step separately in order to have him really expand his ability to do it on his own. Intervention would start out very simple. Sample follows:

1.   Are you listening?

> *Aide:*   Joe, are you listening? [After each question, wait for a response.]
>
> *Aide:*   Who is talking?
>
> *Aide:*   Do you hear her [or the teacher's name]?
>
> *Aide:*   You are looking over here, but you are hearing her.

Have this conversation several times over a week. If he does not start turning himself around to face the teacher then go to next step.

2.   You are listening?

> *Aide:*   Joe, are you listening?
>
> *Aide:*   I don't think the teacher knows.
>
> *Aide:*   You are turned away from her.
>
> *Aide:*   The teacher can't tell you are listening when you are turned away.

Have this conversation several times over a week. If he does not start turning himself around to face the teacher then go to next step.

3.   Show her you are listening.

> *Aide:*   Let's show the teacher that you are listening.
>
> *Aide:*   Let's turn your body toward the teacher to show her you are listening.

The big picture behind this is an effort to help Joe to respond to minimal cueing, and eventually be able to be aware on his own.

Reporting requirements

The child or aide may fill out a checklist to measure how the day has gone for the child. It is important that this be clear ahead of time. The continuity will help the child. It will also show Joe's reaction to changes (e.g., a substitute teacher).

Child's Weekly Schedule

Description

This document should list any resource specialist, speech and language therapy or occupational therapy services regularly scheduled during the week. The schedule could be a simple list or a sample calendar with days across the top and times down the left hand side, depending on the complexity of services provided and child's schedule.

Purpose

The schedule should inform the teacher or substitute so that there will not be confusion or missed appointments.

Responsible party

Could be written up at the annual IEP meeting or at update meetings as the schedule of services changes.

Weekly Schedule (Example)

Monday 9:30 – pragmatic language group in resource room – 45 min. session. Thursday 10:30 – occupational therapist comes to child's classroom for 45 min. session.

Occupational Therapy Interventions

Description

OT interventions used to help the child in specific and general situations (some may also be included in the general overview). If interventions for the child are not available, a general list of useful approaches could be used. Those that do not seem helpful can be crossed off and stars placed by the items that do work. A list of interventions that have worked for the child could also be used.

Purpose

To provide specific interventions to help the child be more successful in school activities. These strategies may help with classroom management and help the student be more successful. OT interventions may help the child improve a skill while working on a project. They may help the child perform better as a member of the classroom by using strategies to deal with sensory processing difficulties.

The goals of interventions may include improvement of a specific motor skill or learning strategies to deal with being overwhelmed in a large group. There may be interventions that are used daily, or used only when specific problems arise.

Responsible party

Written by an occupational therapist (district or private), if possible. If the child has not had intervention in this area, a general list could be obtained with successful interventions noted and unsuccessful ones crossed off the list. Parents may employ strategies at home that they can suggest for use in the school setting. There may be other individuals who have valuable insight into the child and could provide suggestions.

Specific occupational therapy interventions (examples)

FIDGETING

1. A weighted lap pad will be provided for use in the classroom to address Joe's fidgeting in his chair for seated activities.

2. Have Joe stretch his arms up into the air when he is leaning his head on his desk or his forearm. When he moves his feet around underneath the table, it is recommended that he use his own hands to press down on his knees.

3. During circle time, deep pressure to his shoulders may help to organize him. A movement break inside or outside the classroom may help as well. Chewing gum during circle is also recommended.

WRITING

1. Joe may require verbal cueing to use his pencil grip correctly. By telling him to "look for the 'R'," he knows to place his thumb on the "R." This will assist him in using a proper grasp for writing tasks.

2. For writing tasks, Joe should be permitted to tall kneel instead of sitting at times. He fidgeted less when this was attempted in the classroom.

3. For writing tasks, it is recommended that he always use lines, modifying the task to include lines, if necessary. This will increase his attention to lines and spacing. Placing one's finger above the dotted line may serve as a physical prompt to increase his attention to lines.

(A list of general interventions provided by an OT or even from a book can be included for reference, if they seem relevant to this child's issues.)

Speech and Language Interventions

Description

Specific speech and language interventions to be used at school to help the child in specific and general situations. Some of the interventions might also be included in the general overview. If interventions for the specific child are not available, a general list of useful approaches could be used, with things that do not seem to work crossed off and stars placed by those that do work. A running list of things that have worked for the child could also be used in place of a formal list.

Purpose

To provide specific interventions to help the child be more successful in school activities. Having strategies for the teacher to utilize during school may help classroom management significantly and help the student be more successful. The interventions may help the child understand the steps required to complete a project more clearly or help the child communicate and interact better with his peer group.

The goals may include less frustration for the student and teacher as well as improved interactions at school. Interventions may be used daily or when problems arise.

Responsible party

Written by a speech and language therapist (district or private), if possible. If the child has not had intervention in this area, a general list could be obtained with successful interventions noted and unsuccessful ones crossed off the list. Parents may employ strategies that could work in the school setting. There may be other individuals who have valuable insight into the child's communication and could provide suggestions.

Specific speech and language interventions for this child

DIRECTIONS

- Determine if Joe is aware that directions will be given, or cue him.
- Provide directions of five words or less when possible.
- Provide one (or another number) of directions at a time.

- Check for understanding without providing the information at first, such as

  "Joe, What did Mrs Smith ask you to do?"
  "What is the next step?"

INFORMATION

- Tell Joe to listen for information. Ask him or tell him the topic.

- Ask Joe what information was given. What is (was) the topic. What did Mrs Smith say about it?

BEHAVIOR AS COMMUNICATION

- First, ask Joe what he is doing (e.g., yelling, pushing). Tell him if he cannot or does not say.

- Ask him to use words.

- If he does not use words, give him some words or phrases, such as "Tell Johnny to please move," or "Please stop, I don't like when you—."

List of Contacts

Description

List of all the individuals, either provided by the school district or provided privately, involved with the child. The list can include the teacher, aide, occupational therapist, speech and language therapist, resource specialist, psychologist, social worker, SELPA (Special Education Local Plan Area) representative, etc. It would include individuals involved with the IEP and services provided by the district and by the parents. The list could include the name (with parental permission) and the role in the intervention, when this is appropriate for informational purposes. This would not constitute permission for those involved to contact those on the list unless the proper forms were filled out (e.g., district personnel would not contact a private psychologist without a parent of the child filling out a consent form). Phone numbers can be included, when appropriate.

Purpose

To have a comprehensive list so that everyone knows who is involved. The goal is to simplify discussions about the child.

Responsible party

This list could be compiled and then maintained at the annual IEP meeting. Changes and additions could be made, as appropriate, throughout the year.

Current Individual Educational Program (IEP)

Description

Copy of the current IEP forms. (Specific items most relevant to daily interventions could be highlighted.)

Purpose

To have an accessible copy of the document that guides the child's program.

Responsible party

The forms are written and then maintained at the IEP and progress meetings. The person responsible for the overall maintenance of the reference binder could add forms as needed.

Progress Forms

Description

For some children, forms are used to keep track of the child's progress. These forms might be completed daily, weekly, or monthly by the student, aide or teacher. Progress forms can be a tool to systematically track trends, while making it easier to focus on the goals of the intervention, not just the appearance of meeting the goal. The forms would be customized to fit one or more of the IEP goals and the associated intervention strategies. Progress forms would only be utilized: if they make it easier for the child to observe his behavior and progress; if they make it easier for the team to implement the IEP and interventions strategies; or if they provide a significant, systematic support to tracking progress.

Purpose

To make it easier to evaluate what interventions are working and what progress is being made toward a specific goal that might be difficult to measure.

Responsible party

Progress forms may be developed by a member or members of the intervention team and modified as necessary.

General Article about Child's Issue

Description

This is written material that gives a general overview of the issues affecting the child. It could be a copy of a magazine article or a web page that gives a general sense of the challenge. It would not be something that someone wrote specifically for the reference binder. There could be several articles if that gives a more thorough description. This would not be an exhaustive account of the issues. If the parents provide the article(s), they could highlight areas that closely relate to their child.

Purpose

To provide the teacher or aide simple background, right from the start.

Responsible party

IEP team or parent.

Related Websites and Books

Description

List of references for someone interested in learning more about the child's special needs. Try to have some reference books that provide teachers with strategies to address the related special needs.

Purpose

To provide easy access to more information about the child's needs for the interested teacher or aide.

Responsible party

References suggested by members of the intervention team could be compiled by the parent or other person responsible for assembling and maintaining the binder.

Related Terms

Description

A list of general definitions regarding the special needs. It could be one list for all special needs children or one for the particular child (i.e., Asperger Syndrome).

Purpose

To make communication regarding the special needs easier.

Responsible party

The reference binder assembler or contributor.

Possible Interventions and Support Approaches

Description

A list of possible interventions and a sample of each to give a reasonable understanding of how they are to be used. Something that would provide a general sense of what could be used so that the teacher or intervention team could determine if an approach might be successful.

Purpose

To provide easy access to other intervention ideas.

Responsible party

The reference binder assembler or contributor.

Possible interventions and support approaches (examples)

Details or examples could follow each.

SOCIAL STORIES

A simple story written to specifically fit a situation that can explain transitions, cause and effect of behavior, or any other issue that continues to arise.

PEER GUIDANCE

Rotating playground buddy during recess, or lunch and recess, in order to foster appropriate interactions and play during unstructured time.

ENVIRONMENTAL SUPPORTS

Schedules, completion guidelines, support for sensory overload (quiet room, quiet corner).

VISUAL SUPPORTS

Icon schedule if transitions are stressful, etc.

Guidelines and Ideas for Communication

Description

A set of clear guidelines for:

(a) Communication with parent, teacher and parent, aide and parent.

(b) Communication with others:

- teacher and aide
- teacher and other support personnel (occupational therapists, speech and language therapists, resource specialist, etc.)

The guidelines should not restrict communication, but make the process more clear in order to avoid misunderstandings or miscommunications.

Purpose

To have both formal and informal communication that is effective and easy to maintain. To have a process that everyone understands in order to foster the flow of information.

Responsible party

There should be district-wide guidelines and ideas for communication. The actual means of implementing the guidelines might be somewhat modified by individual schools. (These guidelines may already exist.)

District Resource List

Description

List of people to contact in the district if a question arises regarding an issue. List would include SELPA, occupational therapy department, etc.

Purpose

To have an accessible copy of the document that guides the child's program.

Responsible party

SELPA or the resource specialists probably already have one of these lists.

Narrative Regarding IEP Process

Description

A narrative that explains what the process is from start to finish: who begins the process, when to start to meet the deadline, who is involved, who does each part of it, who should be there, what things are included in the IEP, time requirements, when do reassessments occur.

This could include everything that a new teacher would need to know about the process if she had a student with an IEP. It would include information on when the IEP team meets throughout the year.

Purpose

To make sure there is a clear understanding of the who, what, when, where and why of the process in order to make it easier to implement. Additionally, with greater understanding, it may be easier to create and implement IEPs.

Responsible party

A summary of district or state guidelines can be utilized. (The district may have guidelines that it gives to teachers.)

Appendix of Forms

Description

Forms that have been shown to be useful in tracking performance from day to day, month to month, etc. If appropriate, the teacher would be able to choose a form to help monitor trends, track performance and progress toward IEP goals in a simpler way. Include a behavior plan example, if appropriate.

Purpose

To give teachers some additional resources to help track performance to IEP goals.

Responsible party

The reference binder assembler.

References

American Psychiatric Association (1994) *Diagnostic and Statistical Manual of Mental Disorders*, 4th ed. Washington, DC: American Psychiatric Association.

Attwood, Tony (1998) *Asperger's Syndrome: A Guide for Parents and Professionals.* London: Jessica Kingsley Publishers.

Baron-Cohen, S., Leslie, A.M. and Frith, U. (1985) 'Does the autistic child have a "theory of mind"?' *Cognition 21*, 37–46.

Bellugi, U. (2001) (Stimuli and drawings for global and local processing) © Dr Ursula Bellugi, The Salk Institute for Biological Studies, La Jolla, CA 92037.

Bihrle, A.M., Bellugi, U., Delis, D. and Marks, S. (1989) 'Seeing either the forest or the trees: dissociation in visuospatial processing.' *Brain and Cognition 11*, 37–49.

The Dinner Game (1998) (a movie). France: Gaumont (released in the USA by Lion's Gate).

Experimental Education Unit (1995) *Samantha: A Story about Positive Behavioral Support* (a videotape). Washington, DC: Experimental Education Unit, Center on Human Development and Disability, University of Washington, Box 357925.

Frith, U. (1989) *Autism: Explaining the Enigma.* Oxford: Blackwell.

Gray, C. (1994) 'The social story kit.' In C. Gray (ed) *The Original Social Story Book.* Arlington, TX: Future Horizons.

Gray, C. (2000) *The New Social Story Book: Illustrated Edition.* Arlington, TX: Future Horizons.

Happé, F. (October 21, 1997) 'Autism: understanding the mind, fitting together the pieces.' London: Francesca Happé and Mindship International. (www.mindship.org/happe.htm)

Holliday Willey, L. (1999) *Pretending to be Normal.* London: Jessica Kingsley Publishers.

Lotspeich, L. (2001) 'Recognizing and understanding Asperger's Syndrome in your clinical practice.' Presentation at the Cleo Eulau Center Continuing Education Symposium, 3 November.

Milton Bradley Company (1979) *Connect Four* (a game for two players). Milton Bradley Company.

Mitchell, P. (1997) *Introduction to Theory of Mind Children, Autism, and Apes.* London: Arnold.

Silberman, S. (December, 2001) 'The geek disease.' *Wired*, 174–83. (www.wired.com).

Thompson, S. (1997) *The Source for Nonverbal Learning Disorders.* East Moline, IL: Linguasystems.

Ungame Company (1975) *The Ungame* (a board game).

Wheelwright, S. and Baron-Cohen, S. (2001) 'The link between autism and skills such as engineering, maths, physics and computing.' *Autism 5*, 2, 223–7.

Winnicott, D.W. (1965) *The Maturational Process and the Facilitating Environment.* New York: International Universities Press.

Winnicott, D.W. (1992) *The Child, the Family, and the Outside World.* London: Perseus.

Index